Arthur Quiller-Couch

Poems and Ballads

Arthur Quiller-Couch

Poems and Ballads

ISBN/EAN: 9783744712163

Printed in Europe, USA, Canada, Australia, Japan

Cover: Foto ©Thomas Meinert / pixelio.de

More available books at **www.hansebooks.com**

POEMS

AND BALLADS BY

'Q'

SEVERAL of the numbers in this volume have made their first appearance elsewhere; some in *The Speaker*, others in *The Pall Mall Magazine*, others in certain works of fiction published by Messrs. Cassell and Company. Two—*The Splendid Spur* and *The White Moth*—I have taken leave to reprint from a previous volume of verse (*Green Bays: Verses and Parodies*, 1893), and set here in more suitable company. I here acknowledge my indebtedness to the editors and publishers concerned. Q.

CONTENTS

CONTENTS

UPON NEW YEAR'S EVE

Now winds of winter glue
　　Their tears upon the thorn,
And earth has voices few,
　　And those forlorn.

And 'tis our solemn night
　　When maidens sand the porch,
And play at *Jack's Alight*
　　With burning torch,

Or cards, or *Kiss i' the Ring*—
　　While ashen fagots blaze,
And late wassailers sing
　　In miry ways.

Then, dear my wife, be blithe
　　To bid the New Year hail,
And welcome—plough, drill, scythe,
　　And jolly flail.

For though the snows he'll shake
　　Of winter from his head,
To settle, flake by flake,
　　On ours instead;

Yet we be wreathèd green
　　Beyond his blight or chill,
Who kissed at seventeen,
　　And worship still.

We know not what he'll bring:
　　But this we know to-night—
He doth prepare the Spring
　　For our delight.

UPON NEW YEAR'S EVE

With birds he 'll comfort us,
  With blossoms, balms, and bees,
With brooks, and odorous
  Wild breath o' the breeze.

Come then, O festal prime !
  With sweets thy bosom fill,
And dance it, dripping thyme,
  On Lantick hill.
          .

West wind, awake ! and comb
  Our garden, blade from blade—
We, in our little home,
  Sit unafraid.

SABINA

THE stair was steep; the Tower was tall;
    Sabina's strength was gone:
She leaned a hand against the wall,
    And let her boy run on.

High in the blue the Old Tower swayed
    His bells to the sunset breeze:
But ever like hemlock climbed the shade
    Of earth on his earth-hewn knees.

The Widow watched the red sun's glow
    Steal up by the window's edge;
She saw the darkened green below,
    And the wan sheep by the hedge.

SABINA

'Child ! Child !' she called, and 'Wait for me !'
  But ever the boy's feet ran ;
And up through the Whisp'ring Gallery
  Came the voice of her dead man—

'He will not turn for any prayer,
  Nor pause for any tear :
The winds of God harp down the stair,
  Their pinnacle notes ring clear.'

She said, 'My pulse runs low and low :
  He has leapt inside of me.
Blood of my blood, shall he not know
  My blood's necessity ? '

The dead man said, 'He will not wait.
  High in a naked room
A maiden listens, strong as fate,
  And selfish as the tomb.

5

' Her sisters, as they cross the floor,
    Throw glances at the clock :
Her father fumbles with the door,
    He knows he may not lock :

' Her mother pins the bridal crown,
    And pricks her trembling thumbs :
But the bride has laid her mirror down,
    Her small foot drums and drums.

' A minute—hark !   Ah joy, ah joy !
    The helpless door falls wide,
The harp of God and the laugh of a boy
    Sing aubade to the bride.

' The bride she rises from her chair—
    Now never stretch your hands !
The harp, the voice, the climbing stair—
    Naught else she understands.

SABINA

' Follow the harp, take hands and run !
 High on the shining leads,
Or ever a midsummer night's begun
The swallow twitters her orison
 By the granite martyrs' heads ! '

' Dead man, we too have kissed and climbed.
 Inert you moulder there,
And here I fail and flutter, limed
 Fast on the middle stair.

'Sure as upon the still-drawn east
 The evening arch invades ;
Sure as we hold a green earth leased
 Briefly between two shades ;

They will not reach,'
       ' But they will run,
 And hand in hand admire
Through loftier panes an ampler sun,
 List a diviner choir :

7

'Other horizons, widening slopes—
  Yet not a blossom there
But gat its increase from the hopes
  We two were used to share!

'Woman, consign you with the years;
  Consign and follow me.
What though the sun shine on our tears,
  If he the rainbow see?'

The stair was steep; the Tower was tall;
  Sabina's strength was gone:
She bowed her face unto the wall,
  And let her boy run on.

DOOM FERRY

BOATMAN, have they crossed? 'Not all:
  The inn, there, hath an upper chamber,
And a window in the wall
  Where the small white roses clamber.

' Many shelves run round the room ;
  On a shelf, and no man near them,
Two are talking low i' the gloom—
  From the trellis' foot may'st hear them.'

Who are they? 'At dawn they came
  By the Passage, calling *Over !*
She the corpse of a comely dame,
  And the man, methinks, her lover.'

Boatman, land and climb the stair :
   By the scented window-boxes
Lower me that loving pair
   Here among the crimson phloxes.

Boatman, is this honey-dew
   Dripping from the window-boxes ?
Nay, I cannot tell its hue
   Here against the crimson phloxes.

Take a guinea and a groat :
   One in ale shall keep thee merry ;
Let the other fee the boat
   Tiding these across the ferry.

Take this purse : it shall persuade
   Him who digs i' th' acre yonder
Them to bed with a cunning spade
   Cheek by jowl, no turtles fonder.

DOOM FERRY

Cheek by jowl, and heart by heart,
    But a thought in either buried,
That shall push them wide apart—
    Wide enough ere a third be ferried.

So, between, my body I'll thrust,
    Laughing, straightening out my knees there,
Either hand in a little dust
    Dabbling, at my cool dead ease there.

A HOUSEKEEPING

Surprised by young desire, as by the dawn,
  A young Orion, wildered, half awake,
Bedraggled, drenched in woodland ways withdrawn,
  My heart, a-tiptoe by a dewy brake,
    Spied the gods sleeping—vision of green lawn,
    Pale ivory limbs, pillows of dappled fawn,
      And a great quiet, and a stilly lake.

There the long grasses topped a banquet spread
  —For that the turf had been their only table—
With cates and fruit and delicate white bread,
  Roses a-float in craters carved with fable.
    There droop'd a wreath from each relaxèd head,
    And there on garland and on god were shed
      The coverlet of years innumerable.

A HOUSEKEEPING

They perish not, beneath the secular oak—
  Olympian Jove and all his greenwood train :
And yet no breath heaves any purple cloak ;
  Yet the thin leaves list on their lips in vain ;
    In vain the veils of morning, like a smoke,
    Shake with the spiral lark. Be whist, invoke—
      They perish not, yet will not live again.

Anon upon that lake a shudder swept,
  And therewithal a feeble childish wail ;
And lo ! a naked wingèd babe that stepped
  Shoreward atween the weed and galingale,
    And sought the whitest queen of all, and crept
    Close to her side, and clapped her cheek, and wept,
      And coaxed her ear with many an elfin tale.

' Mother, awake ! The Western Wind arrives !
  Down the long gulf he breaks a wavering stair
For Phœbus' gilded feet, and shoreward drives,

And sings across the meadows, debonair,
　　Pelting the Heaven with dust of golden hives,
　　Blown saffron bloom, and small birds with their
　　　　wives,
　　　　And happiness in handfuls everywhere.

' Late as I couched high on the Latmian cliff,
　　I heard the red pine whisper wakefully ;
I saw the pasturing brood-mare pause and sniff
　　The salt newcomer ; and with mainsail free
　　　　A helmsman hailed me from his bobbing skiff—
　　　　' Praise the West Wind !' How shall I praise
　　　　　　him, if,
　　　　　　If, Cytherea, he awake not thee ?

' He may adorn the day ; but ah ! the dark—
　　The dark destroys me ! When the shepherds fold
And hie them, each to his confederate spark,
　　His window lit, his beacon on the wold,

Then lie they warm.   But me the house-dog's bark
Drives houseless, quaking through the midnight
    park :
  All creatures love, but Love himself's a-cold !'

Thereat I stepped and gently him bespake—
  ' Dear child, my cottage hath an empty room,
A flask of thin wine and an oaten cake.
  She, an she wake, will thank me—She, for whom
    Kings left their loves, them blithely to betake
    To war, the while that for her lovely sake
      Wild War himself laid by his lance and plume.'

Then first he started back a little space ;
  But after came and laid a hand in mine,
As glad of one that spake his mother's praise.
  So forth we fared : and happy our design,
    Till *thou* cam'st fluttering through the forest ways,
    Thou, with the woodland sunburn on thy face,
      Thou, in green kirtle pinned with eglantine.

15

'Hillo!' criedst thou, 'what darling leadest there?
  Come, pretty chuck!'—and heaped him kiss on
    kiss.
'An orphan? Save thee from his mannish care!
  Fond foundling, say, what do men know of this?'
    'But he is mine,' said I; 'unless thou share—'
    'If thou,' she falter'd, 'hast but room to spare—'
      Fool, fool, fool heart! sub-letting so thy bliss!

Thenceforward for a month, as shines in Lent
  The mead with daffodils, my cottage shone
With days and nights-made-noonday, being spent
  In serving him that first had made us one.
    And then, as droop in April's discontent
    Those daffodils, thy will declined, and went
      Forth from my door, leaving us there alone.

Ah, had we never met—or, having met,
  Had I been wiser or thy heart less wild!

For, wanting thee, at first he 'gan to fret,

And then to hunger as a weaning child :

And perished, wanting thee.   Aud yet—and yet—

Hadst thou but turned or showed the least regret,

How had he waked, and stretched his arms,

and smiled !

SHADOWS

As I walked out on Hallows' E'en,
I saw the moon swing thin and green ;
I saw beside, in Fiddler's Wynd,
Two hands that moved upon a blind.

As I walked out on Martin's Feast,
I heard a woman say to a priest—
' His grave is digged, his shroud is sewn ;
And the child shall pass for his very own.'

But whiles they stood beside his tomb,
I heard the babe laugh out in her womb—
' My hair will be black as his was red,
And I have a mole where his heart bled.'

THE MASQUER IN THE STREET

MASQUER on the rainy stones,
  Jigging, twirling 'neath the rain,
Wherefore shake thine aged bones
          To that antique strain ?

Limp thy locks and lank and thinned,
  Thy grey beard it floats a yard ;
And thy coat tails flap i' the wind
          Like a torn placard.

'Hush !' saith he ; 'there was a House—
  From its porch the cressets flared ;
Lads in livery called "Carouse !
          For thy lust 's prepared ! "

19

' Like a snake the prelude wound—

    Crash ! the merry waltz began :

One unto my mind I found,

        And our feet ran.

' Rubies ripped from altar-cloths

    Leered adown her silk attire ;

Her mad shoes were scarlet moths

        In a rose of fire.

' Tropic scents her tresses weaved—

    Scents to lay the soul a-swoon ;

On her breast the draperies heaved

        Like clouds by the moon.

' Back she bent her throat, her wet

    Southern lips, and dared, and dared—

Over them my kisses met,

        While the saxe-horn blared.

THE MASQUER IN THE STREET

'Crash ! the brassy cymbal smote—
   When I would have stayed our feet,
Laughter rippled all her throat
      Like a wind on wheat.

'Every laugh it left a crease,
   Every ripple wrote her old—
Yet her arms would not release,
      Nor her feet with-hold.

'Ah ! to watch it suck and sag—
   Rosy flesh 'had breathed so warm—
Till I twirled a loveless hag
      On a tortured arm !

'Dancers, resting for a while
   Down the wall with faces white,
Watched us waltzing, mile on mile,
      In a horror of light !'

Masquer on the rainy stones,

   What is that thy fingers fold?

' Dead or dying, naught atones

      But I dance and hold.

' Crash! the maddened cymbal smote—

   Are they minutes?   Are they years,

That I hold but dust to my coat

      And a few gold hairs?'

Masquer in the rainy close,

   God thee pity and thy bone!

Other men have danced with those,

      And now dance alone.

DOLOR OOGO

THIRTEEN men by Ruan Shore,
    —Dolor Oogo, Dolor Oogo—
Drownèd men since 'eighty-four,
    Down in Dolor Oogo:
    On the cliff against the sky,
    Ailsa, wife of Malachi—
      That cold woman—
    Sits and knits eternally.

By her silent husband's side
    — Dolor Oogo, Dolor Oogo—
Stretched awake, she hears the tide
    Moan in Dolor Oogo:

Till athwart the easter gale

Hark ! the merry dead men hail—

'Thou cold woman,

Take the lantern from the nail ! '

Rising in her chilly sark

—Dolor Oogo, Dolor Oogo—

Forth she fares by Behan Parc,

Out to Dolor Oogo :

Kneeling there above the brink,

Lets her long red tresses sink

—That cold woman—

For the sailor men to drink.

Then the sailor men beneath

—Dolor Oogo, Dolor Oogo—

Take the ends between their teeth,

Deep in Dolor Oogo.

DOLOR OOGO

‘ Lusty blood is this to quaff :

(So the merry dead men laugh)

O, cold woman,

Hath thy man as good by half? ’

‘ Drownèd men by Ruan Shore

      —Dolor Oogo, Dolor Oogo—

Lost aboard the *Elsinore*

      Down by Dolor Oogo—

If the gulls behind the share

Yesterday had called “ Beware,

      Thy cold woman ! ”

Paler now had been my hair.

‘ Socks I knit you each a pair

      —Dolor Oogo, Dolor Oogo—

Half of yarn and half of hair,

      Over Dolor Oogo.’

‘ Dripping, dripping on the tide,

What red dye thy hair hath dyed,

Thou cold woman ? ’

‘ It hath brushed upon his side.’

Knitting with her double thread

—Dolor Oogo, Dolor Oogo—

Half of black and half of red—

Over Dolor Oogo,

On the cliff against the sky,

Ailsa, wife of Malachi,

That cold woman,

Wipes her hands incessantly.

ODE

UPON ECKINGTON BRIDGE, RIVER AVON

I

O PASTORAL heart of England! like a psalm
　Of green days telling with a quiet beat—
O wave into the sunset flowing calm!
　O tirèd lark descending on the wheat!
Lies it all peace beyond that western fold
　Where now the lingering shepherd sees his star
Rise upon Malvern?　Paints an Age of Gold
　　Yon cloud with prophecies of linkèd ease—
　　Lulling this Land, with hills drawn up like knees,
　To drowse beside her implements of war?

II

Man shall outlast his battles.   They have swept
  Avon from Naseby Field to Severn Ham ;
And Evesham's dedicated stones have stepped
  Down to the dust with Montfort's oriflamme.
Nor the red tear nor the reflected tower
  Abides; but yet these eloquent grooves remain
Worn in the sandstone parapet hour by hour
    By labouring bargemen where they shifted ropes.
    E'en so shall man turn back from violent hopes
To Adam's cheer, and toil with spade again.

III

Ay, and his mother Nature, to whose lap
  Like a repentant child at length he hies,
Not in the whirlwind or the thunder-clap
  Proclaims her more tremendous mysteries :
But when in winter's grave, bereft of light,

UPON ECKINGTON BRIDGE, RIVER AVON

With still, small voice divinelier whispering

—Lifting the green head of the aconite,

    Feeding with sap of hope the hazel-shoot—

    She feels God's finger active at the root,

Turns in her sleep, and murmurs of the Spring.

SONNET

ISLES OF SCILLY

I saw Narcissus in a portico
   Leaning his ear toward the yellow bells
   Of his own flower, festooned, that from the shells
Voluted, on the pavement, caught the low
Long echoes of an Archipelago
   Afar, beyond the pillared parallels
   Wherein a soft wind wound, and nothing else,
Between his shoulder and the afterglow.

Figure of bronze !   Thou listenest alway :
   Ever for thee that lazy song beguiles.
But I must wake, and toil again, and pray ;
   And yet will come but rarely, and at whiles,
The shout and vision of the sea-gods grey,
    Stampeding by of the lone Scillonian isles.

VICTORIA

(June 22nd, 1893)

' There was absolutely no panic, no shouting, no rushing aimlessly about. The officers went quietly to their stations. Everything was prepared, and the men were all in their positions. . . . I can further testify to the men below in the engine-rooms. . . . In all the details of this terrible accident one spot especially stands out, and that is the heroic conduct of those who to the end remained below, stolidly yet boldly, at their place of duty.'—*Captain Bourke's Statement.*

Queen ! What is this that comes

Borne on thy rolling drums

At sunrise from the far

Syrian borders ?

—Sped from the flags that fly

Half-mast at Tripoli,

Where float the ships of war,

Thy virgin warders ?

31

Where tarries she who should
Captain that sisterhood,
　　Named with thy name, and own
　　　　Offspring of Victory ?
Deep, eighty fathoms deep,
She, with her crew asleep,
　　Recks not the signal flown,
　　　　Vain, valedictory.

Not in Thy day of wrath,
Lord God of Sabaoth,
　　Nor upon rock or sand
　　　　Hemmed with Thy breath round ;
But leading tranquilly
Upon a tranquil sea,
　　Swift at a sister's hand
　　　　Took she her death-wound.

VICTORIA

Launched on the fatal curve,

Too late to stay or swerve,

    Starkly the *Camperdown*

        Rounded, descended,

Struck—saw, and backward reeled,

As he who on the field

    By Oxus smote his own

        Sohrab, the splendid.

But She, the stricken hull,

The doomed, the beautiful,

    Proudly to fate abased

        Her brow Titanic.

Praise now her multitude

Who, nursed in fortitude,

    Fell in on deck and faced

        Death without panic.

Heaven, that to admirals,

Assigns their funerals,

  To some the battle's ridge

    Full-starred, to die on—

Took not the spirit proud

From him she less allowed.

  —Calm, cool, upon the bridge,

    Sank the brave Tryon !

Now for the seamen whom

Thy not degenerate womb

  Gave thus to die for thee,

    England, be tearless :

Rise, and with front serene

Answer, thou Spartan queen,

  ' Still God is good to me :

    My sons are fearless.'

VICTORIA

Back to the flags that fly
Half-mast at Tripoli,
   Back on the sullen drum
      Mourning *Victoria*,
Loud, ay, and jubilant,
Hurl thine imperial chant—
   ' *In morte talium*
      Stat Matris gloria !

THE SPLENDID SPUR

Not on the neck of prince or hound,

Nor on a woman's finger twined,

May gold from the deriding ground

Keep sacred that we sacred bind :

Only the heel

Of splendid steel

Shall stand secure on sliding fate,

When golden navies weep their freight.

THE SPLENDID SPUR

The scarlet hat, the laurelled stave,
    Are measures, not the springs of worth ;
In a wife's lap, as in a grave,
    Man's airy notions mix with earth.
        Seek other spur
        Bravely to stir
The dust in this loud world, and tread
An Alp among the whisp'ring dead.

Trust in thyself,—then spur amain :
    So shall Charybdis wear a grace,
Grim Ætna laugh, the Libyan plain
    Take roses to her shrivelled face.
        This orb—this round
        Of sight and sound—
Count it the lists that God hath built
For haughty hearts to ride a-tilt.

THE COMRADE

STRANGER by the tavern board,
   Brown man with the splendid eyne,
Thou and I make no accord
   Till thou give the countersign
   Here, across the Rhenish wine.

I had word in Trebizond
   Of thy favours to my blood,
Of my father's cancelled bond,
   Why his widow lacked not food:
   Truly I believe thee good.

Well I know my mother's lips
   Called thee kinder than her Own
In those months my wandered ships,
   Fouler than this red beard grown,
   Wallowed in a raving zone.

THE COMRADE

'Needs no token round thy neck !—
    Over desert's dusky white,
When the frosted quarter-deck
    Shivered back the Northern Light
    Through the aching Arctic night ;

By the coral-locked lagoon,
    While upon the seamless blue
Like a silver clasp, the moon
    Drew the gauzèd night, wherethrough
    Her two horns dripped honey-dew ;

Thine the face that, first and last,
    Haunted me.   For thee I scanned
Passing deck and distant mast,
    Peep of dawn and lift of land.
    Now we meet—hold back thy hand !

Though thou smilest by the board,
    And our fingers itch to twine,

Thou and I make no accord
   Till I have the countersign
   Here, across the Rhenish wine.

He that loves but half of Earth
   Loves but half enough for me.
Succourer of starving Worth,
   Say, but could thy Charity
   Stoop as pitiful a knee,

Hold as equable a torch
   O'er the hell that sinners tread?
Tenderly, in windy porch,
   Lift the drooping harlot's head,
   As the good man's in his bed?

Earth, that built our jolly bones,—
   Earth, that brewed our jovial blood,—
In each atom of us owns

THE COMRADE

Spark of filial fire that should
Quicken to the parent mood.

Here, astride the paps of Earth,
　With the wind upon thy face,
Canst resound thy mother's mirth,
　Catch a breath and say a grace
　For the glory of the pace ?—

Thankful for thy privilege
　In the hunter's gallant stride,
In the glancing rapid's edge,
　In the waters that divide
　To thy nimble, naked pride;

Thankful for the climber's heel
　Fast above the smooth ravine,
For the hand-shake of the wheel,
　When the giddy royals lean
　And the forefoot treads it green;

For the sleep of tirèd limbs,
  For the taste of meat and wine,
For the merry laugh that brims
  Labour as with a froth divine ;—
  Pledge me this, and I am thine.

Then to horse !—the gates are wide.
  Host, a cup before we go !
He and I are pledged to ride
  Till the gust of onset blow
  Dead the failing spark ; and so,—

Having reached, or failed to reach,
  In no Abbey will we lie,
But upon a league-long beach
  Find the braver cemet'ry,
  Sweetened by the wave and sky.

THE CAPTAIN

THERE is a captain that commands,
    And never but to victory :
' The counsel of thine heart it stands,
    No man so faithful unto thee.'
      Though seven senses watch the wall,
      And all thy courage leap at call,
      He is thine ark and arsenal,
        Thine armour and artillery.

Yea, while the cloakèd sentries tramp
    And challenge with a deep ' All 's well ! '
He lists the sappers from the camp
    Encroaching on thy citadel ;

43

Invisible he tries the guns,

And leaning o'er the bastions

Discerns the tented legions,

    Earthwork and trench and parallel.

O man ! in vain they creep and mine ;

  Thy ramp remains inviolate.

But if by folly or design

  Thou force thy friend to abdicate,

    A broken pole, a trodden keep,

    The standard of thy soul shall weep,

    And all her trophies lie a heap

      That owls and satyrs desecrate.

COLUMBUS AT SEVILLE

DEAR son, Diego, I am old and deaf:
Here to my room in Seville some one came
— To-day or yesterday, who knows? The blinds
Are closed, and no sun moves upon the floor—
Here to my room in Seville some one came
And muttered that the queen is dead. I trust
She rests in glory, far from all the cares
Of this rough world she made less penible
For two much-travelled feet that here inert
Wait by the ripple of the Blessed Ford,
Yet may not to its running cool unlace
Until my Master give the happy word.

I have been loyal: flouted for a fool,
I have been loyal: lifted above lords,

45

I have been loyal : once again abased,

Beggared and led a prisoner in chains,

I have been loyal still.   But I believe

God sets on kings His sigil for a test,

And only they who bear it to His bourne

By widows' tears uncancelled, without scratch

Of fetters wrongfully imposed, undimmed

By sighs of just petitioners, may claim

To hear their charter yonder reconfirmed.

Who fails—his province shall another take,

One chosen from the spirits of just men

Made perfect.   And his own debt shall every one

Here or hereafter, soon or late, redeem.

Who plights his dignity against a debt,

As Ferdinand ; who thus evades a debt,

As Ferdinand, and forfeits faith of man ;

Shall find that faith confront him by the Throne

In angels' blushes, and his honours melt

For payment in their slow celestial scorn.

COLUMBUS AT SEVILLE

But she, my Mistress, diadem of all

His dignity, was never Ferdinand's.

Born of that royal few who ride abroad

And see their humbler, happier sisters throw

Free glances from their windows on the street ;

Or by the bridge or by the bathing-pool

Passing with nun-like faces, catch a hint

And bear it home and wonder all the night

Stretched by their lords, listing the serena e

That well by distant balconies passionate ;

She—though her priestess' body she abased

Coldly to public need—lent it to wed

Castille with Aragon—was dedicate

To none but duty.   On this earth she knew

No passion but a friendship purified,

Unspotted of the flesh, prophetical

Of that sublimer passion of the saints

Her innocence now inherits.—Not for me !

As not for Ferdinand !   But this I hope,

To meet her walking 'neath the boughs of Life,

To touch her hand without servility,

And in the salutation of her eyes

Read resolution of the musing care

That clouded them aforetime, half with doubt

And half with pitiful knowledge.

                    Oh, they swept

Down from the daïs eloquent, wave on wave

In every wave brooded a starry thought;

In every thought brooded a litten tongue,

Holy, with comfortable words.   And yet

I have looked into them as a mother looks,

And in the iris of her week-old babe

Reads now but natal innocence, and now

The absorbèd wisdom of an age-worn past

Blinking its own new dawn.   They did allow

The wonder of man's weakness, even while

They pierced unto his greatness and the hope

Natheless at first I did believe her cold

—Jesu! She cold!—cold as the icèd rim

'Engaged my hot heart there by Pinos bridge.

Tight-corded as my holster was the bale,

The slender bale of hope I carried then,

If somewhere I might find the world so wide

As to contain one courage bold to mate

With me to push it wider—wide enough

To satisfy the more adventurous clans

Yet in the womb waiting the moment's call.

For Portugal had cheated, England sent

No word, and of Bartholomew no report

Came on the bearded lips of them who drew

Forth from the northern fogs in caravel,

Galley or barque or pinnace. Day by day

For two long years, seated among my books,

Maps, charts, and cross-staves, in the little shop

By Seville bridge, incessant I had watched

The Guadalquiver through a dusty pane;

Had watched the thin mast creep around the point;

Had watched the slow hull warp across the tide,

And the long flank fall lazy to the quay

—Levantine traders bringing Tyrian wine,

Malmsey from Crete, fine lawn of Cyprus, silk

Of Egypt and of India.   Genovese,

Whose sheer I conned and knew the shipwright's name,

—Feluccas, with a world of eastern spice

Bartered of Caspian merchants on the bar

Of Poti, or of Emosaïd clans

Down the Red Sea and south to Mozambique :

True aloes of Socotra, galbanum,

Myrrh, cassia, rhubarb, scented calamus,

Sweet storax, cinnamon, attars of the rose

And jasmine.   And of some the skippers wore

Skin purses belted underneath their knives

—Spoilers of Ormuz or of Serendib,

Who sought the jeweller's offices ere they slept

Or drank ashore.   These from the sunrise all :

But others from the dark and narrow seas

By England and by Flanders.   Tin they brought

In blocks and bars, and lead and pewter ware

Shipped at Southampton.   Lace and napery

Of Ypres and of Malines, Frankish wools

In bulk from Calais' warehouses, or spun

By English hands, grey kersey, fustian, cloth,

From Guildford, Norwich, London.—

                                      Ay, but none

Brought tidings of Bartholomew.   One and all,

Still to my questioning the shipmen stared

And shook their silver earrings : not a word !

Oft—as th' Orcadian watcher from his rock

Scans the grey tide-race eddying by his line—

In tavern corner by an empty cup

I have heard the roboant captains boast and swell ;

Alert, if haply, on vainglorious tale

Or outland lie reported, there might drift

Some flotsam of the dim West unexplored.

Bird of my hope! How long ye beat a wing

In yon unfathomable fogs, and still

Of green no sign!—the waters ever void,

And empty the pink feet of Noë's dove!

At Salamanca then they tested us;

Churchmen and schoolmen and cosmogoners

In council. 'Hey!' and 'What?' 'The earth a
    sphere?

And two ways to Cathaia?' 'Tut and tush!'

'Feared the Cathaians then no blood in the head

From walking upside-down?' 'Pray did I know

Of a ship 'would sail up-hill?' 'Had I not heard

Perchance of latitudes when the wheel of the sun

Kept the sea boiling? Of the tropic point

Where white men turned hop-skip to blackamoors?'

'And hark ye, sir, to what Augustine says,

And here is Cosmas' map. *" God built the world*

COLUMBUS AT SEVILLE

As a tabernacle: sky for roof and sides,
And earth for flooring . . . Made all men to dwell
Upon the face of it "—the face, you hear,
Not several faces—*" On foundations laid*
The earth abides"—foundations, if you please,
Not mid-air.   Soothly, sir, at your conceits
We smile, but warn you that they lie not far
On this side heresy.   "Antipodes," hey?
Our Mother Church annuls the Antipodes.'

Fools, fools, Diego !   Ay, but folly makes
More orphans than malevolence.

                     There I stood
Rejected, and the good queen looked on me.
She did not smile.   Thank God she did not smile
She did not speak.   I saw the mute lips move
Compassionate, and took defeat, went forth.

Nay, no compassion now !   With scorn of men
I bound my wound, and nursed it while I rode.

France now, or England? Still the wound complained,

And still I closed the purple lips with scorn;

Till there on Pinos bridge my horses hoof

Rang, and the vaulted echo halloa'd 'Scorn!'

And so—

        I do remember, on a time,

Off Cape St. Vincent in a general fight,

How that one master of a sinking hull

—An Antwerp captain—danced about his deck

Like paper in a gale, and cursed and bawled,

And cursed again and shook his fist and bawled,

Belabouring his gunners—fat and fierce

As a fool's bladder, wholly ludicrous;

Till running to the bulwarks, all aflush

To hurl some late-remembered oath, he leaned,

Collapsed in bloody vomit, and so died.

So with the bridge's echo welled afresh

My wound above its bandages.   I lit

COLUMBUS AT SEVILLE

Down from my horse and o'er the parapet bowed

In sickness of surrender ; let my hopes

Unhusk and rain upon the silly stream

That ran ecstatic, with a babbling lip

A-flush for the salt tide, and knew not yet

The smart of that embrace.   'Run, happy fool !

Aspire to make impression on the main,

'Will swallow thee with all thy freshet wave

As kings digest the tributary zeal

Of private men, and so spit forth their names.'

So leaned I, listless to a gallop of hoofs

'Woke distant on the north-east road and swept

Down in a smother of dust.   I sprang to the bit,

And backed to let the posting rider past.

But he reined sudden and wheeled.   'Why this will be

—Steady, thou sprawler !—this will be the man,

The Genovese himself !   Sir, I have ridden—

The queen commands you back to Santa Fé.

Plague o' this dust !'   I looked him up and down :

A little dapper gentleman of the camp,

Flicking with scented kerchief at his coat

Of velvet laced with amber, like a bee's,

And condescending with a silly smile.

And still he smiled ; and still I pondered him,

As a father, listening in his closet, hears

The first cry of his first-born child, and turns

To watch an idle bee upon the pane,

And still in the midwife's message hears it buzz.

'The queen commands—' 'So—I believe you, sir' :

Then slowlier : 'And I will trust the queen.'

With eyebrows lifted, and a brisk salute,

He shook his rein, dug spur, and started back

A-trot with the answer.

　　　　　　　Haste, O bobbing bee !

Be minister of marriage 'twixt two minds,

Two flowers that twine the challenge of their gaze

And know no fleshlier union.   Soar, O bee !

COLUMBUS AT SEVILLE

Hence from the moat up, up to the lady-flower

Swaying in sunlight high on the palace wall ;

Creep in her leaning languid bosom, and there

Do thy close work, whisper, impregnate her

With a secret such as lowlier blossoms breathe

At twilight, one to another, nodding anigh

With petalled nightcaps, while th' eaves - dropping

    breeze

Steals by the lily-bordered garden beds.

Nay ; 'tis a chaster deed thou hast in hand

—To marry mind with mind.   Stand but afar

And speak : thou hast a word that not alone

Will breed conception of a queenly thought,

But wake the generations of the world.

Dame of the castle !   Leman of the road !

Leap with the quickening babe and press your side !

He hath the resurrection in his heel,

Treads underfoot the doom of all his sires,

And springs upon the tight cords wherewithal

In turn they bound each other to the pit.

Dame of the castle !   Leman of the road !

Enlarge your girdles !—for this conquering babe

Shall westward launch and draw with silver wake

An honourable girdle round the waist

Of Mother Earth, beneath her swelling breasts—

The Old World and the New.   O moons of man !

A Spirit moves upon the middle deeps,

And all their odic tides acclaim the Babe !

Back then I rode : but coolly Reason came

With sight of Santa Fé, and plucked my arm—

' Be temperate : for kings have many cares

And thou one vision only.   See these walls,

These tented lines ; and yonder on the cliff,

At her last gasp, Granada.   Tranquilly,

As 'twere on oilèd hinge, the sentinel

Paces her terrace.   Evening for her wounds

Hath golden ointment, were they curable.

But at their meat the dusky councillors
Mutter "To-morrow!" and upon the wall
The whisperers surmise.   "To-morrow?   Ay—
There dawns one only morrow for the Moor!"
But O, what blood! O man, what many blows
Have built that morrow!   Christendom redeems
The debt, attains the dream.   O give her space,
A kindly space before she dream again!'

Soberly then I cleansed me of the dust
Of travel; stood within the royal tent
With brow composed.   And she with brow composed
Questioned my hope as 'twere i' the level round
Of a queen's audience.   Cold?   I did not know
She had sought to pledge her jewels for that hope!
Only her tone took up the challenge flung
By my obeisance, challenging in turn
Her Court, as who should say, 'Behold this man,
He offers a new heaven, a new earth;

And claims to hold them for us, taking tithe
As Governor, and for his share one-eighth
Of his adventure's profit, with the style
Of Admiral of the Ocean, privilege
As high as our High Admiral's of Castile :
Well worth it, an his promises bear fruit.
I test him at the furthest of his claim—
Go, sir—so much an unbelieving world
Concedes its queen : derisive lets her launch
Fresh hopes forlorn upon its unbelief—
Go, sir, and prove the courage of thy faith.'

And Faith, my son, the substance is of things
Hoped for, the evidence of things not seen.
The substance ? ay, I trod it ! not the deck,
The barren deck whereon my comrades cursed
The wind, the smooth sea running like a stream
Still westward, westward through an empty world.
Nay, while they cursed, my feet already pressed

COLUMBUS AT SEVILLE

The yellow sands, waded the rivulets

And long cool grasses of those isles afar.

The evidence? I saw it! not the weed,

The crab, the berried branch, the emperor-fish,

The tropic birds that sang about the mast

As 'twere a sweet-briar bursting into bud

In Seville, in the Andalusian spring.

—Signs and a *sursum corda* for the faint

And faithless.   Sudden then a few would crowd

Forward, and point, and hail the dull blue smear

Far on the sky-line.   'News, Lord Admiral!

A land-fall, ho! and luck be with the news!'

—So watch it fade, and curse more bitterly.

Me neither hope nor omen, true or false,

Elated or depressed.   Always I bore

The certainty within me, and the seal

Of God upon it, and the face imposed

Of her, my Mistress.   Always on the poop,

A man apart, I stood and steered a course

Unerring, by the magnet of my doom.

Others might watch, all eager for the prize—

The thirty annual crowns and velvet coat—

For veritable sight and news of land.

The *Pinta* might outsail, the *Nina* balk

Their Admiral.   But still for him reserved

The hour, and for his eyes the blessed light,

The light on Guanahani!   Musing there,

Through the first watch, beside the cabin top,

I heard between me and the hornèd moon

A frigate-bird go whistling, and a wind

Caught in the rigging like a woman's sigh :

Whereat I turned——O face !   O flash of eyes !

O star of my devotion ! all dissolved

Into a spark that danced and disappeared,

And dancing glowed again, as 'twere a torch

Moved in a village street from door to door.

I called the watch.   They had not seen : but ran,

Stared, saw—'Land! land!' and 'Praise the Admiral!

Who found us light in darkness? Who but he?'

—More proof? Then rede thee of that bitter gale

Off the Azores, on the homeward road.

The *Nina* drove alone in seas that drowned

Hope and the very heaven. There we cast

Lots who should carry—barefoot, in his sark—

A candle to Our Lady of Guadelupe.

Who drew the lot but I? Again we cast.

And who but I the pilgrim to Moguer,

To Santa Clara? Yea, yet once again

A night of anguish off the Tagus mouth ;

Again the lot ; again the Admiral !

Me must Our Lady of La Cinta choose :

There was none other. Proofs? I tell thee, son,

There was none other ! These men handled ropes,

Starved, hoped, shed tears—mechanical, for me

Their master. As I meted them, they moved.

But Pinzon—who betrayed me once and twice

At Cuba—thought us foundered in the gale,

Nor stayed to search; but made his hope, his shame,

Both doubled by desertion—who, with sail

Piled high as both, let drive the *Pinta* home

To bear the first report and snatch the prize—

I swear I pitied him.   How like to mine

His hope, if mine had lacked the single grace

Made his contention impotent! lacking which,

He smote upon a consecrated shield

That on the stroke rang God's authentic 'No!'

Thou knowest how upon a mid-day tide

We drew unto that port of our desire ;

To Palos, little Palos, left so long,

After what wonders found! and all the roofs

Rocked, and the mist of faces on the quay

Heaved, and the anchor dropped, and home was home.

Thou knowest how, that moment looking back,

We saw a lean hull creeping past the bar—

The *Pinta*!—never spoken since the Azores !

COLUMBUS AT SEVILLE

And Pinzon—traitor, by an hour too late !

Always I pitied him.   He had designed

To post to Barcelona with the news :

Now heard the royal mandate, 'Never come

But with the Admiral thou shouldst have served.'

Whereat he turned him to his native town,

To his own house ; there on the threshold pushed

By wife and children, mounted to his room,

And turned the key, and knew his hour, and died.

But my reward, how came it ?

                      Proud enough

That hour in Barcelona ; the April sky

Shaken with bells and cannon and flame of flags ;

The cheers, the craning heads, the blossoms thrown

And kerchiefs from the windows fluttering,

Flock after flock, like doves let forth to greet

The dusty golden pageant—Juan first,

The Pilot, with the Standard of Castile :

E   65

The slow brown Indians in their feather cloaks

And paint: the seamen bearing fruit and palms,

Parrots and gold-fish, conchs and turtle-shells,

Lizards on poles, lign-aloes, trays of spice,

And gold in calabashes: last of all

The Admiral.   So, they led me to the throne,

Where she and Ferdinand rose, as to a prince,

And hardly would permit me kiss their hands:

But seated me beside them, bade me tell

All our adventures—rarely smiled the Queen—

' Yea, all,' she said.   In the great circle's hush,

Beneath the canopy of cloth-of-gold,

I found my voice and spake—' Most Catholic King,

And thou, Star-regent of our enterprise,

Sooner than half were told, this April night

Would shake the planets from her dusky wings

Down-hovering.   Yet an hour shall tell enough

To tune all tongues to anthems praising God.'

So for an hour I told the tale; and twice

COLUMBUS AT SEVILLE

Paused : but insistent she commanded ' More ! '

Leaning with parted lip and kindling cheek,

As might the Carthaginian, had no drought

Of passion parched her dusky throat, have leaned

To Troy's immortal wanderer.   Was it then

Came my reward ?

                      Not then, nor ever so.

But long years after, when that dream was grey,

And the heart wise, and fellowship was none

(For 'tis the curse of greatness, to outgrow

All friends and from the lone height long for friends,

And falling, find the friends it left all gone),

—Years afterward, when black was favour's torch

And faith took bribes ; when Ferdinand betrayed,

And Bobadilla, High Commissioner,

Foamed at his lunatic height, raged like a beast,

Cast us in chains, shipped us like beeves to Spain—

Then, from the pit of that most brutal fall

A voice commanded 'Break his chains!   He shall
In person stand before us, plead his cause.'
Carefully then I dressed me as became
The Admiral of the Ocean.   Squire and page
And retinue—I did abate no jot
While the purse bled.   A prince, and all a prince,
I passed between the sneering chamber crowd,
The whispering abjects of the ante-rooms,
Into the presence : stood there, cold, erect.
' I am Columbus.   I have left my chains
Nailed at my bed's head by the crucifix :
And come to know what further, O my King ? '
Then Ferdinand—I saw him bite his lip—
Sat with pink face averted.   But the Queen
Rose from her throne, silent—I would have knelt ;
Too late !   She stretched her hands and, silent
     yet,
Gazed, and the world fell from us, and we wept—
We two, together . . .

Ah, blessed hands! Ah, blessed woman's hands—

Stretched to undo irreparable wrong!

Yea, the more blest being all impotent!

A queen's I had not touched: but hers met mine

In humbleness across man's common doom,

In sadness and in wisdom beyond pride.

They are cold beside her now, and cannot stir.

Further than I have travelled she hath fared:

But I shall follow. Soon will come the call:

And I shall grip the tiller once again.

The purple night shall heave upon the floor

Mile after mile; the dawn invade the stars,

The stars the dawn—how long? And following
down

The moon's long ripple, I shall hear again

The frigate-bird go whistling—see the flash—

The light on Guanahani! Salvador!

Let thy Cross flame upon me in that star,

And from that Cross outstretch *her* sainted hands!

My son, they tell me that the Queen is gone.

I trust she rests in glory, free from all

The cares of this rough world.   She was my friend :

And I shall find it harder now to treat

With Ferdinand.   He fends me off with words.

I thought that last petition ill prepared ;

And have an ampler one ; drawn up and signed

To-day, or yesterday—who knows ?   The blinds

Are closed, and no sun moves upon the floor.

THE WHITE MOTH

IF a leaf rustled, she would start :
  And yet she died a year ago.
How had so frail a thing the heart
  To journey where she trembled so ?
And do they turn and turn in fright,
  Those little feet, in so much night ?

The light above the poet's head
  Streamed on the pane and on the cloth,
And twice and thrice there buffeted
  On the black pane a white-winged moth :
'Twas Annie's soul that beat outside
  And 'Open ! open ! open !' cried :

' I could not find the way to God :
   There were too many flaming suns
For signposts, and the fearful road
   Led over wastes where millions
Of tangled comets hissed and burned—
   I was bewildered and I turned.

' Oh, it was easy then !   I knew
   Your window and no star beside.
Look up, and take me back to you !'
   —He rose and thrust the window wide.
'Twas but because his head was hot
   With rhyming : for he heard her not.

But poets polishing a phrase
   Show anger over trivial things ;
And as she blundered in the blaze
   Towards him, on ecstatic wings,
He raised a hand and smote her dead ;
   Then wrote, ' *That I had died instead !* '

PREMONITION

SHE sat upon the cottage stair,—
  A tender child of three,
And washed and dressed with wisest care
  The doll upon her knee.

And we, who guessed not why there grew
  In Annie's baby eyes
That little clouding of the blue,
  That shade of awed surmise,

Remembered, in the darkened room,
  Where yesterday we took
Our Annie's new-born babe, on whom
  Her eyes might never look.

HELFORD RIVER

SONG

HELFORD RIVER, Helford River,
　　Blessed may ye be !
We sailed up Helford River
　　By Durgan from the sea.

O to hear the hawser chain
　　Rattle by the ferry there !
Dear, and shall we come again
　　By Bosahan,
By wood and water fair ?

All the wood to ransack,
　　All the wave explore—
Moon on Calamansack,
　　Ripple on the shore.

HELFORD RIVER

—Laid asleep and dreaming
  On our cabin beds;
Helford River streaming
  By two happy heads;

—Helford River, streaming
  By Durgan to the sea,
Much have we been dreaming
  Since we dreamed by thee.

Dear, and shall we dream again
  The one dream there?
All may go if that remain
  By Bosahan,
And the old face wear!

'TO THE LAND WHERE YE GO . .

To the land where ye go
   Ye may not beckon me ;
In the ranks ye shall know
   Ye shall not reckon me.
On the earth ye did move
As deep below as high above
   All your surroundings.
I cast a plummet in your love
   And found no soundings.

Pools of heaven were your eyes ;
   Their deeps rejected not
One whom wide Paradise
   Pitied, reflected not.

'TO THE LAND WHERE YE GO . . .'

Was it time lost to lean

My longing lip toward the clean

Well-springs of healing,

Surprise the soul mine might have been,

And ponder, kneeling?

TO BEARERS

Maids, carry her forth—your dead,
   Your pale young queen ;
Two at her feet, two at her head,
   And four between.—
Not as we wanted it,
But as God granted it.

Not now to the swinging chime,
   To the organ swell,
Keep we the rank, treading in time—
   But one dull bell.
Open the gates for her !
The Bridegroom waits for her.

TO BEARERS

We never had dreamed it so :

    But she—she knew ;

Walking aloof, placid of brow

    Her short life through

Scornful, in surety

Guarding her purity.

Buds born for the bridal path

    Cover her breast :

Babes of the dream now that she hath

    Sleep in her rest.

Our peace above her let

Fall for her coverlet.

THE GENTLE SAVAGE

Go down, my Soul, unto the river ;
 The day is done, the mountain mute ;
Thou hast a message to deliver—
 Why loiterest yet irresolute ?
  See, on the farther bank,
  The lamp-light winking
Across the city, cooling there her flank
  Like a beast drinking.

Down by the mill, the ghostly miller
 May see a twilit phantom steal
And loose an arrow duskier, shriller,
 Than flies the bat about his wheel.

THE GENTLE SAVAGE

Arrow of secret call!

Call to her only

Who, at her window on the city wall,

Waiteth so lonely.

O mother, in thy royal chamber

How barest thou such a son as I?

Thou, cased at heart with pearl and amber,

With starch and stiff embroidery:

I, the brown Ishmaelite—

I, whom the starry

Summits behold at loose upon the night

After my quarry?

Small mother mine, amid thy roses

Thy heart sings all the day content.

The curtained wall that round thee closes

Reminds not of imprisonment.

I, on the mountain-tops
All the day roaming,
Recall thee never till a shadow drops
From the rook, homing.

That call renews our blood's confusion—
Thy babe leaps naked back to thee:
Thy soul remembers her seclusion,
And mine abhors her liberty.
Suppliant I nestle then
To thee the stronger,
And seek my strength of thee, mother of men,
Mere queen no longer.

A moment, and our wiser senses
Restore to each the life apart.
Yet, as the violet condenses
All Venus in one dewy heart,

THE GENTLE SAVAGE

So all the night I hear
Thy lids distilling
A love that holds in every purple tear
Love's planet thrilling.

THE PLANTED HEEL.

By Talland Church as I did go,
I passed my kindred all in a row ;

Straight and silent there by the spade
Each in his narrow chamber laid.

While I passed, each kinsman's clay
Stole some virtue of mine away :

Till my shoes on the muddy road
Left not a print, so light they trod.

Back I went to the Bearer's Lane,
Begged the dead for my own again.

THE PLANTED HEEL

Answered the eldest one of my line—
'Thy heart was no one's heart but mine.'

The second claimed my working skill,
The third my wit, the fourth my will :

The fifth one said, 'Thy feet I gave ;
But want no fleetness here in the grave.'

'For feet a man need have no care,
If they no weight of his own may bear.

'If I own naught by separate birth,
What binds my heel e'en now to the earth ?'

The dead together answered back—
'Naught but the wealth in thy knapsack.'

'Nay, then,' said I, 'that's quick to unload' :
And strewed my few pence out on the road.

'O kinsmen, now be quick, resume
Each rag of me to its rightful tomb!'

The dead were silent then for a space.
Still I stood upright in my place.

Said one, 'Some strength he will yet conceal.'
'Belike 'tis pride of a planted heel?'

'Man has but one perduring pride:
Of knowledge alone he is justified.

'Lie down, lie down by us in the sod:
Thou shalt be wise in the ways of God.'

'Nay, so I stand upright in the dust,
I'll take God's purposes all on trust

'An inch of heel for a yard of spine,
So give me again the goods that are mine!'

THE PLANTED HEEL

I planted my heel by their headstones,
And wrestled an hour with my kinsmen's bones.

I shook their dust thrice into a sieve,
And gathered all that they had to give.

I winnowed knowledge out of the heap :
'Take it,' I said, 'to warm your sleep.'

I cast their knowledge back on the sod,
And went on my journey, praising God.

Of all their knowledge I thought me rid :
But one little grain in my pack had hid.

Now, as I go, myself I tell—
'On a planted heel man wrestles well.'

But that little grain keeps whispering me—
'Better, perhaps, on a planted knee.'

87

IA'S SONG

Long before day I left my father's cottage,
I went by the tamarisks upon the hedges by the sea,
Seeking my lovely one, my comforter, before the
    morning.

My brothers three lie drowned by Dolor Oogo.
They call in the night: 'Little sister, when is the
    wedding?
It is cold waiting, and thou a drudge in our father's
    cottage.'

Now must I go and whisper them 'Not yet'—
Not yet; but the thyme of the hedge kisses my naked
    foot—
So will he kiss me soon, and comfort me, my pretty
    lover.

IA'S SONG

Then will I kneel by him, and he shall bandage

The wounds of the brambles, and I, kneeling beside

him,

Softly, my arm holding his waist, will kiss him—ah,

when?

A FIDDLER'S VALENTINE

Pretty player, from thy strings
Little whispers take them wings—
   Take them wings and hie to me !
In my hollow heart they dwell
Swinging it as 'twere a bell
   Ding-a-ding inside o' me.
Hand to play and heart to ring—
Together might they make a spring
On earth beyond imagining :
   But nay, and nay—
   For now my love's denied to me.
Therefore, dear, lay down thy fiddle,
Clip me once around the middle,
   Kiss, and say good-bye to me !

THE KERCHIEF

WHEN I 'gan to know thee, dear,
  Thy faults I did espy;
And 'Sure this is a blemish here,
  And that's a blot,' said I.

But from that hour I did resign
  My judgment to my fate,
Thou art no more than only mine
  To love and vindicate.

The kerchief that thou gav'st I wear
  Upon mine eyelids bound,
And every man I meet I dare
  To find the faults I found.

LOVE SEQUESTERED

THOUGH in her grey unclouded eyes
No cheat abode, nor compromise,
But truth in clearest outline shone,
And sin from honour stood alone ;

Yet to be with her was to walk
A faëry shore, and list the talk
Of dropping streams, and nightingales,
And gods dissolved in inland vales.

And though we loved and lived remote,
Nor feat achieved deserving note,
Each trivial step was sanctified
In that we took it side by side.

THE LEAST OF THESE

' Lord, in Thy Courts

    Are seats so green bestow'd,

As there resorts

    Along the dusty road

A cavalcade,—King, Bishop, Knight, and Judge :

And though I toil behind and meanly trudge,

Let me, too, lie upon that pleasant sward,

    For I am weary, Lord.

' Christ, at Thy board

    Are wines and dishes drest

That do afford

    Contentment to the best.

93

And though with Poverty my bed hath been

These many years, and my refreshment lean,

With plenty now at last my soul acquaint,

    Dear Master, for I faint.'

    But through the grille,

      ' Where is thy Robe ? ' said He

    ' Wouldst eat thy fill,

      Yet shirk civility ? '

' My Robe, alas !   There was a little child

That shivered by the road——' Swiftly God smiled :

' I was that Child,' said He, and raised the pin ;

    ' Dear friend, enter thou in ! '

CAROL

Fling out, fling out your windows wide '
   I bring you joy this Christmas-tide:
To-day is born in Bethlehem
A son of royal David's stem :
   Then sing and rest you satisfied—
           In excelsis gloria !

' Where is the royal Babe arrayed ? '
   Lo ! He is in a manger laid ;
The Lord of life an ox's guest—
But warm He lies on Mary's breast ?
   Then sing and rest you undismayed.

' How may we find His manger-bed ? '

   There shines a star above His head ;

And choirs of viewless Cherubin

Shall guide you to that humble inn :

   Then sing and rest you comforted.

' And is it He that should be sent ? '

   Three kings came from the Orient

A-riding with the tokens three

From Ind, Cathay, and Arabye :

   Then sing and rest you confident.

' What bringeth He, this new-born King ? '

   Lo ! all good gifts there are to bring.

'Tis He shall turn your tears to mirth,

And send goodwill and peace on earth :

   Then kneel, and rest you worshipping—

         In excelsis gloria !

CHILD'S CAROL

NAKED boy, brown boy,
  In the snow deep,
Piping, carolling
  Folks out of sleep;
Little shoes, thin shoes,
  All so wet and worn—
But I bring the merry news
  —Christ is born!

Rise, pretty mistress!
  Don a gay silk;
Give me for my good news
  Bread and new milk.

Joy, joy in Jewry,
   This very morn !
Far and far I carry it
   —Christ is born !

Back, back in Bethl'em,
   By the moon still,
There I saw a shepherd
   Sitting on a hill :
' Boy,' said he, ' bonny boy,
   Take you this horn,
Wend you now and wind it,
   —Christ is born !

And whenever people
   Hear the merry blast,
Bells in every steeple,
   Flags on every mast,

CHILD'S CAROL

Holy boughs and holly
    Adore and adorn,
Far and far and jubilant
    —Christ is born!

Therefore I would have you
    People comprehend
Christ is born in Bethl'em
    For to be your friend:
For to bear the agony,
    For to wear the thorn,
For to die on Calvary,
    —Christ is born!

HOLY INNOCENTS

Us Herod slew,

Willing to slay the infant Christ, our Lord.

But from the sword

Our tender life in globes of lighted dew

Trickled and twinkling ran

Before Him to the waste Egyptian,

Gilding His way like glow-worms on the sward.

Now in His house

He draweth us to deck the Christmas fir

From chest of myrrh ;

Whom as Aunt Mary bindeth on the boughs,

Her eyes drop happy rain

For sorrow past—and lo ! we live again

As babies trembling in the tears of her.

JETSOM

WHERE Gerennius' beacon stands
High above Pendower sands ;
Where, about the windy Nare,
Foxes breed and falcons pair ;
Where the gannet dries a wing
Wet with fishy harvesting,
And the cormorants resort,
Flapping slowly from their sport
With the fat Atlantic shoal,
Homeward to Tregeagle's Hole—
Walking there, the other day,
In a bight within a bay,
I espied amid the rocks,
Bruised and jammed, the daintiest box
That the waves had flung and left

101

High upon an ivied cleft.

Striped it was with white and red,

Satin-lined and carpeted,

Hung with bells, and shaped withal

Like the queer, fantastical

Chinese temples you 'll have seen

Pictured upon white Nankin,

Where, assembled in effective

Head-dresses and odd perspective,

Tiny dames and mandarins

Expiate their egg-shell sins

By reclining on their drumsticks,

Waving fans and burning gum-sticks.

Land of poppy and pekoe !

Could thy sacred artists know—

Could they possibly conjecture

How we use their architecture,

Ousting the indignant Joss

For a pampered Flirt or Floss,

JETSOM

Poodle, Blenheim, Skye, Maltese,

Lapped in purple and proud ease—

They might read their god's reproof

Here on blistered wall and roof,

Scaling lacquer, dinted bells,

Floor befouled of weed and shells,

Where, as erst the tabid Curse

Brooded over Pelops' hearse,

Squats the sea-cow, keeping house,

Sibylline, gelatinous.

Where is Carlo? Tell, O tell,

Echo, from this fluted shell,

In whose concave ear the tides

Murmur what the main confides

Of his compassed treacheries !

What of Carlo? Did the breeze

Madden to a gale while he,

Curled and cushioned cosily,

Mixed in dreams its angry breathings

With the tinkle of the tea-things

In his mistress' cabin laid?

—Nor dyspeptic, nor dismayed,

Drowning in a gentle snore

All the menace of the shore

Thundered from the surf a-lee

Near and nearer horribly,—

Scamper of affrighted feet,

Voices cursing sail and sheet,

While the tall ship shook in irons—

All the peril that environs

Vessels 'twixt the wind and rock

Clawing—driving?   Did the shock,

As the sunk reef split her back,

First arouse him?   Did the crack

Widen swiftly and deposit

Him in homeless night?

                Or was it,

Not when wave or wind assailed,

JETSOM

But in waters dumb and veiled,
That a looming shape uprist
Sudden from the channel mist,
And with crashing, rending bows
Woke him, in his padded house,
To a world of altered features?
Were these panic-ridden creatures
They who, but an hour agone,
Ran with biscuit, ran with bone,
Ran with meats in lordly dishes,
To prevent his lordly wishes?
But an hour agone!   And now how
Vain his once compelling bow-wow!
Little dogs are highly treasured,
Petted, patted, pampered, pleasured :
But when ships go down in fogs,
No one thinks of little dogs.

Ah, but how dost fare, I wonder,

Now thine Argo splits asunder,

Pouring on the wasteful sea

All her precious bales, and thee?

Little use is now to rave,

Calling god or saint to save ;

Little use, if choked with salt, a

Prayer to holy John of Malta.

Patron John, he hears thee not.

Or, perchance, in dusky grot

Pale Persephone, repining

For the fields that still are shining,

Shining in her sleepless brain,

Calling, ' Back ! come back again ! '

Fain of playmate, fain of pet—

Any drug to slay regret,—

Hath from hell upcast an eye

On thy fatal symmetry,

And beguiled her sooty lord

With his brother to accord

JETSOM

For this black betrayal.   Else

Nereus in his car of shells

Long ago had cleft the waters

With his natatory daughters

To the rescue : or Poseidon

Sent a fish for thee to ride on—

Such a steed as erst Arion

Reached the mainland high and dry on.

Steed appeareth none, nor pilot !

Little dog, if it be thy lot

To essay the dismal track

Where Odysseus half hung back,

How wilt thou conciliate

That grim mastiff by the gate ?

Sure 'twill puzzle thee to fawn

On his muzzles three that yawn

Antrous ; or to find, poor dunce,

Grace in his six eyes at once—

Those red eyes of Cerberus.

Daughters of Oceanus,

Save our darling from this hap !

Arethusa, spread thy lap,

Catch him, and with pinky hands

Bear him to the coral sands,

Where thy sisters sit in school

Carding the Milesian wool :—

Clio, Spio, Beroe,

Opis and Phyllodoce,—

Pass by these, and also pass

Yellow-haired Lycorias ;

Pass Ligea, shrill of song—

All the dear surrounding throng ;

Lay him at Cyrene's feet

There, where all the rivers meet :

In their waters crystalline

Bathe him clean of weed and brine,

Comb him, wipe his amber eyes,

Then to Zeus who rules the skies

JETSOM

Call, assembling in a round
Every fish that can be found—
Whale and merman, lobster, cod,
Tittlebat and demigod :—
'Lord of all the Universe,
We, thy finny pensioners,
Sue thee for the little life
Hurried hence by Hades' wife.
Sooner than she call him her dog,
Change, O change him to a mer-dog !
Re-inspire the vital spark ;
Bid him wag his tail and bark ;
Bark for joy to wag a tail
Bright with many a flashing scale ;
Bid his locks refulgent twine,
Hyacinthe, hyaline ;
Bid him gambol, bid him follow
Blithely to the mermen's 'halloa !'
When they call the deep-sea calves

Home with wreathèd univalves.

Softly shall he sleep to-night,

Curled on couch of stalagmite,

Soft and sound, and scarcely moister

Than the shell-protected oyster.

Grant us this, Omnipotent,

And to Hera shall be sent

One black pearl, but of a size

That shall turn her rivals' eyes

Greener than the greenest snake

Fed in meadow-grass, and make

All Olympus run agog—

Grant for this our darling dog !'

Musing thus, the other day,

In a bight within a bay,

I 'd a sudden thought that yet some

Purpose for this piece of jetsom

Might be found ; and straight supplied it.

JETSOM

On the turf I knelt beside it,
Disengaged it from the boulders,
Hoisted it upon my shoulders,
Bore it home, and, with a few
Tin-tacks and a pot of glue,
Mended it, affixed a ledge ;
Set it by the elder-hedge ;
And in May, with horn and kettle
Coax'd a swarm of bees to settle.
Here around me now they hum ;
And in Autumn should you come
Westward to my Cornish home,
There 'll be honey in the comb—
Honey that, with clotted cream
(Though I win not your esteem
As a bard), will prove me wise,
In that, of the double prize
Sent by Hermes from the sea, I 've
Sold the song and kept the bee-hive.

THE BIG REVIEW

(To be sung to a pipe and drum quick-step)

WHEN I went up, a raw recruit,
  To Bodmin town from Scorrier,
Our Colonel wore a gold-laced suit
  Like a warrior all ablaze :
Our Colonel held a Big Review,
  With knapsack, pouch, and bagginet,
An' the Colonel's daughter drove thereto
  In a wagginet drawn by bays.

THE BIG REVIEW

The drums they beat, the trumpets blowed,
 The guns went off impartial ;
But of all the regiment Private Coad
 In a martial way did best.
' Stand forth, stand forth, thou hero bold !
 To you the rest be secon'-rate :
'Tis you shall wear this clasp of gold
 For to decorate your broad chest !—

O where, O where 's my best recruit
 That e'er I paid a shillin' for ? '
—But all the regiment stuck there mute,
 Unwillin' for to explain ;
Till forth I steps, and gives a cough,
 And answers him so dutiful—
' Look, Colonel, dear, he 's gallopin' off
 With your beautiful daughter Jane ! '

'Of all the plans that e'er I 've known,

Says he, 'I do call that a plan

To bring my hairs in sorrow down

With a rataplan to the grave !

Form up, form up, each galliant blade,

Form up, my sons of Waterloo !

I ain't goin' to spoil my Big Parade

For a mortal who can't behave !'

L'ENVOI

Go little book, and this let be thy prayer—
   That critics may consider well, and take
   Thee for thine own and not the writer's sake,
But have of him, apart from thee, no care.

Much have I tried and little have achieved—
   Much have myself dissatisfied with prose,
   Which yet I aimed to better; and, God knows,
Have more myself than any critic grieved.

But thou art separate.   Youngling of my heart
   I cannot judge thee, whether good or bad.
   In doubt thou wast begotten, dearest lad,
And still in doubt I kept thee long apart.

Now at the door, with ribbons in thy cap,

    Doubt not, but draw from these parental eyes

    A double courage for the enterprise.

Go, slender youth : God send thee gentle hap !

NOTES

Page 27.—Where the Avon winds under Bredon Hill in Worcestershire, and just where the Malverns come into view, a bridge of native sandstone crosses between the villages of Eckington and Defford. Its parapet is scored with many deep grooves and notches, worn in the stone by the tow-ropes of departed barges. The river from Tewkesbury to Stratford was made navigable in 1637 by Mr. William Sandys, of Fladbury, 'at his own proper cost.' But railways have ruined waterways: the locks above Evesham have fallen into decay, while those below have lost their custom, and Stratford no longer (in the words of the Rev. Richard Jago, author of *Edge-hill*)—

> ' her spacious magazines unfolds,
> And hails th' unwieldy barge from western shores
> With foreign dainties fraught, or native ore
> Of pitchy hue, to pile the fuel'd grate,
> In woolly stores or husky grain repay'd.'

Page 43, lines 3, 4.—'And let the counsel of thine own heart stand; for there is no man more faithful unto thee than it.

'For a man's mind is sometime wont to tell him more than seven watchmen, that sit above in an high tower.'—ECCLESIASTICUS, xxxvii. 13, 14.

Page 49, line 3.—'Pinos bridge.' There is a tradition that Columbus, broken by the indifference of the Spanish Court, had started to seek aid in England for his project, but was overtaken on the bridge of Pinos by a messenger from Isabella, bearing a fresh promise of assistance. Being urged by the messenger to return to Santa Fé, he pondered and replied, 'I will take the word of the noble queen.'

Page 50, lines 4 and following.—'Levantine traders. . . .' See *The Career of Columbus*, by Mr. Charles I. Elton (1892), p. 15.

Page 56, line 16.—'Be minister of marriage. . . .' I hope the critic will pardon my having put into the mouth of Columbus this anticipation of a quite modern discovery.

Printed by T. and A. CONSTABLE, Printers to Her Majesty
at the Edinburgh University Press

A CATALOGUE OF BOOKS
AND ANNOUNCEMENTS OF
METHUEN AND COMPANY
PUBLISHERS : LONDON
36 ESSEX STREET
W.C.

CONTENTS

OCTOBER 1896

MESSRS. METHUEN'S
ANNOUNCEMENTS

Poetry

RUDYARD KIPLING

BALLADS. By RUDYARD KIPLING. *Crown 8vo.* 6s.

150 copies on hand-made paper. *Demy 8vo.* 21s.
30 copies on Japanese paper. *Demy 8vo.* 42s.

The enormous success of 'Barrack Room Ballads' justifies the expectation that this volume, so long postponed, will have an equal, if not a greater, success.

GEORGE WYNDHAM

SHAKESPEARE'S POEMS. Edited, with an Introduction and Notes, by GEORGE WYNDHAM, M.P. *Crown 8vo.* 3s. 6d.
[*English Classics.*

W. E. HENLEY

ENGLISH LYRICS. Selected and Edited by W. E. HENLEY. *Crown 8vo. Buckram.* 6s.

Also 15 copies on Japanese paper. *Demy 8vo.* £2, 2s.

Few announcements will be more welcome to lovers of English verse than the one that Mr. Henley is bringing together into one book the finest lyrics in our language. The volume will be produced with the same care that made 'Lyra Heroica' delightful to the hand and eye.

'Q'

POEMS AND BALLADS. By 'Q,' Author of 'Green Bays, etc. *Crown 8vo. Buckram.* 3s. 6d.

25 copies on Japanese paper. *Demy 8vo.* 21s.

History, Biography, and Travel

CAPTAIN HINDE

THE FALL OF THE CONGO ARABS. By SIDNEY L. HINDE. With Portraits and Plans. *Demy 8vo.* 12s. 6d.

This volume deals with the recent Belgian Expedition to the Upper Congo, which developed into a war between the State forces and the Arab slave-raiders in Central Africa. Two white men only returned alive from the three years' war—Commandant Dhanis and the writer of this book, Captain Hinde. During the greater part of the time spent by Captain Hinde in the Congo he was amongst cannibal races in little-known regions, and, owing to the peculiar circumstances of his position, was enabled to see a side of native history shown to few Europeans. The war terminated in the complete defeat of the Arabs, seventy thousand of whom perished during the struggle.

S. BARING GOULD

THE LIFE OF NAPOLEON BONAPARTE. By S. BARING GOULD. With over 450 Illustrations in the Text and 13 Photo-. gravure Plates. *Large quarto.* 36*s.*

This study of the most extraordinary life in history is written rather for the general reader than for the military student, and while following the main lines of Napoleon's career, is concerned chiefly with the development of his character and his personal qualities. Special stress is laid on his early life—the period in which his mind and character took their definite shape and direction.

The great feature of the book is its wealth of illustration. There are over 450 illustrations, large and small, in the text, and there are also more than a dozen full page photogravures. Every important incident of Napoleon's career has its illustration, while there are a large number of portraits of his contemporaries, reproductions of famous pictures, of contemporary caricatures, of his handwriting, etc. etc.

It is not too much to say that no such magnificent book on Napoleon has ever been published.

VICTOR HUGO

THE LETTERS OF VICTOR HUGO. Translated from the French by F. CLARKE, M.A. *In Two Volumes. Demy 8vo.* 10*s.* 6*d. each. Vol. I.*

This is the first volume of one of the most interesting and important collection of letters ever published in France. The correspondence dates from Victor Hugo's boyhood to his death, and none of the letters have been published before. The arrangement is chiefly chronological, but where there is an interesting set of letters to one person these are arranged together. The first volume contains, among others, (1) Letters to his father; (2) to his young wife; (3) to his confessor, Lamennais; (4) a very important set of about fifty letters to Sainte-Beuve; (5) letters about his early books and plays.

J. M. RIGG

ST. ANSELM OF CANTERBURY: A CHAPTER IN THE HISTORY OF RELIGION. By J. M. RIGG, of Lincoln's Inn, Barrister-at-Law. *Demy 8vo.* 7*s.* 6*d.*

This work gives for the first time in moderate compass a complete portrait of St. Anselm, exhibiting him in his intimate and interior as well as in his public life. Thus, while the great ecclesiastico-political struggle in which he played so prominent a part is fully dealt with, unusual prominence is given to the profound and subtle speculations by which he permanently influenced theological and metaphysical thought; while it will be a surprise to most readers to find him also appearing as the author of some of the most exquisite religious poetry in the Latin language.

EDWARD GIBBON

THE DECLINE AND FALL OF THE ROMAN EMPIRE. By EDWARD GIBBON. A New Edition, edited with Notes, Appendices, and Maps by J. B. BURY, M.A., Fellow of Trinity College, Dublin. *In Seven Volumes. Demy 8vo, gilt top.* 8*s.* 6*d.* each. *Crown 8vo.* 6*s. each. Vol. II.*

W. M. FLINDERS PETRIE

A HISTORY OF EGYPT, FROM THE EARLIEST TIMES TO
THE PRESENT DAY. Edited by W. M. FLINDERS PETRIE, D.C.L.,
LL.D., Professor of Egyptology at University College. *Fully
Illustrated. In Six Volumes. Crown 8vo. 6s. each.*

Vol. II. XVII.-XVIII. DYNASTIES. W. M. F. PETRIE.

'A history written in the spirit of scientific precision so worthily represented by Dr.
Petrie and his school cannot but promote sound and accurate study, and supply a
vacant place in the English literature of Egyptology.'—*Times.*

J. WELLS

A SHORT HISTORY OF ROME. By J. WELLS, M.A., Fellow
and Tutor of Wadham Coll., Oxford. With 4 Maps. *Crown 8vo.
3s. 6d. 350 pp.*

This book is intended for the Middle and Upper Forms of Public Schools and for
Pass Students at the Universities. It contains copious Tables, etc.

H. DE B. GIBBINS

THE HISTORY OF ENGLISH INDUSTRY. By H. DE B.
GIBBINS, M.A. With 5 Maps. *Demy 8vo. 10s. 6d. Pp.* 450.

This book is written with the view of affording a clear view of the main facts of
English Social and Industrial History placed in due perspective. Beginning
with prehistoric times, it passes in review the growth and advance of industry
up to the nineteenth century, showing its gradual development and progress.
The author has endeavoured to place before his readers the history of industry
as a connected whole in which all these developments have their proper place.
The book is illustrated by Maps, Diagrams, and Tables, and aided by copious
Footnotes.

MRS. OLIPHANT

THOMAS CHALMERS. By Mrs. OLIPHANT. *Second Edition.
Crown 8vo. 3s. 6d.* [*Leaders of Religion.*

Naval and Military

DAVID HANNAY

A SHORT HISTORY OF THE ROYAL NAVY, FROM
EARLY TIMES TO THE PRESENT DAY. By DAVID HANNAY.
Illustrated. Demy 8vo. 15s.

This book aims at giving an account not only of the fighting we have done at sea,
but of the growth of the service, of the part the Navy has played in the development of the Empire, and of its inner life. The author has endeavoured to avoid
the mistake of sacrificing the earlier periods of naval history—the very interesting
wars with Holland in the seventeenth century, for instance, or the American
War of 1779-1783—to the later struggle with Revolutionary and Imperial France.

COL. COOPER KING

A SHORT HISTORY OF THE BRITISH ARMY. By Lieut.-Colonel COOPER KING, of the Staff College, Camberley. *Illustrated. Demy 8vo. 7s. 6d.*

This volume aims at describing the nature of the different armies that have been formed in Great Britain, and how from the early and feudal levies the present standing army came to be. The changes in tactics, uniform, and armament are briefly touched upon, and the campaigns in which the army has shared have been so far followed as to explain the part played by British regiments in them.

G. W. STEEVENS

NAVAL POLICY: WITH A DESCRIPTION OF ENGLISH AND FOREIGN NAVIES. By G. W. STEEVENS. *Demy 8vo. 6s.*

This book is a description of the British and other more important navies of the world, with a sketch of the lines on which our naval policy might possibly be developed. It describes our recent naval policy, and shows what our naval force really is. A detailed but non-technical account is given of the instruments of modern warfare—guns, armour, engines, and the like—with a view to determine how far we are abreast of modern invention and modern requirements. An ideal policy is then sketched for the building and manning of our fleet; and the last chapter is devoted to docks, coaling-stations, and especially colonial defence.

Theology

F. B. JEVONS

AN INTRODUCTION TO THE HISTORY OF RELIGION. By F. B. JEVONS, M.A., Litt.D., Fellow of the University of Durham. *Demy 8vo. 12s. 6d.*

This is the third number of the series of 'Theological Handbooks' edited by Dr. Robertson of Durham, in which have already appeared Dr. Gibson's 'XXXIX. Articles' and Mr. Ottley's 'Incarnation.'

Mr. F. B. Jevons' 'Introduction to the History of Religion' treats of early religion, from the point of view of Anthropology and Folk-lore; and is the first attempt that has been made in any language to weave together the results of recent investigations into such topics as Sympathetic Magic, Taboo, Totemism, Fetishism, etc., so as to present a systematic account of the growth of primitive religion and the development of early religious institutions.

W. YORKE FAUSSETT

THE *DE CATECHIZANDIS RUDIBUS* OF ST. AUGUS-TINE. Edited, with Introduction, Notes, etc., by W. YORKE FAUSSETT, M.A., late Scholar of Balliol Coll. *Crown 8vo. 3s. 6d.*

An edition of a Treatise on the Essentials of Christian Doctrine, and the best methods of impressing them on candidates for baptism. The editor bestows upon this patristic work the same care which a treatise of Cicero might claim. There is a general Introduction, a careful Analysis, a full Commentary, and other useful matter. No better introduction to the study of the Latin Fathers, their style and diction, could be found than this treatise, which also has no lack of modern interest.

General Literature

C. F. ANDREWS

CHRISTIANITY AND THE LABOUR QUESTION. By C. F. ANDREWS, B.A. *Crown 8vo.* *2s. 6d.*

R. E. STEEL

MAGNETISM AND ELECTRICITY. By R. ELLIOTT STEEL, M.A., F.C.S. With Illustrations. *Crown 8vo.* *4s. 6d.*

G. LOWES DICKINSON

THE GREEK VIEW OF LIFE. By G. L. DICKINSON, Fellow of King's College, Cambridge. *Crown 8vo.* *2s. 6d.*
[*University Extension Series.*

J. A. HOBSON

THE PROBLEM OF THE UNEMPLOYED. By J. A. HOBSON, B.A., Author of 'The Problems of Poverty.' *Crown 8vo.* *2s. 6d.*
[*Social Questions Series.*

S. E. BALLY

GERMAN COMMERCIAL CORRESPONDENCE. By S. E. BALLY, Assistant Master at the Manchester Grammar School. *Crown 8vo.* *2s.*
[*Commercial Series.*

L. F. PRICE

ECONOMIC ESSAYS. By L. F. PRICE, M.A., Fellow of Oriel College, Oxford. *Crown 8vo.* *6s.*

This book consists of a number of Studies in Economics and Industrial and Social Problems.

Fiction

MARIE CORELLI'S ROMANCES

FIRST COMPLETE AND UNIFORM EDITION

Large crown 8vo. *6s.*

MESSRS. METHUEN beg to announce that they have commenced the publication of a New and Uniform Edition of MARIE CORELLI's Romances. This Edition is revised by the Author, and contains new Prefaces. The volumes are being issued at short intervals in the following order :—

1. A ROMANCE OF TWO WORLDS.   2. VENDETTA.
3. THELMA.   4. ARDATH.
5. THE SOUL OF LILITH.   6. WORMWOOD.
7. BARABBAS.   8. THE SORROWS OF SATAN.

BARING GOULD

DARTMOOR IDYLLS. By S. BARING GOULD. *Cr. 8vo.* 6s.

GUAVAS THE TINNER. By S. BARING GOULD, Author of 'Mehalah,' 'The Broom Squire,' etc. Illustrated. *Crown 8vo.* 6s.

THE PENNYCOMEQUICKS. By S. BARING GOULD. New Edition. *Crown 8vo.* 6s.

A new edition, uniform with the Author's other novels.

LUCAS MALET

THE CARISSIMA. By LUCAS MALET. Author of 'The Wages of Sin,' etc. *Crown 8vo.* 6s.

This is the first novel which Lucas Malet has written since her very powerful 'The Wages of Sin.'

ARTHUR MORRISON

A CHILD OF THE JAGO. By ARTHUR MORRISON. Author of 'Tales of Mean Streets.' *Crown 8vo.* 6s.

This, the first long story which Mr. Morrison has written, is like his remarkable 'Tales of Mean Streets,' a realistic study of East End life.

W. E. NORRIS

CLARISSA FURIOSA. By W. E. NORRIS, 'Author of 'The Rogue,' etc. *Crown 8vo.* 6s.

L. COPE CORNFORD

CAPTAIN JACOBUS : A ROMANCE OF HIGHWAYMEN. By L. COPE CORNFORD. Illustrated. *Crown 8vo.* 6s.

J. BLOUNDELLE BURTON

DENOUNCED. By J. BLOUNDELLE BURTON, Author of 'In the Day of Adversity,' etc. *Crown 8vo.* 6s.

J. MACLAREN COBBAN

WILT THOU HAVE THIS WOMAN? By J. M. COBBAN, Author of 'The King of Andaman.' *Crown 8vo.* 6s.

J. F. BREWER

THE SPECULATORS. By J. F. BREWER. *Crown 8vo.* 6s.

A. BALFOUR

BY STROKE OF SWORD. By ANDREW BALFOUR. *Crown 8vo.* 6s.

M. A. OWEN

THE DAUGHTER OF ALOUETTE. By Mary A. Owen.
Crown 8vo. 6s.
A story of life among the American Indians.

RONALD ROSS

THE SPIRIT OF STORM. By Ronald Ross, Author of
'The Child of Ocean.' *Crown 8vo. 6s.*
A romance of the Sea.

J. A. BARRY

IN THE GREAT DEEP: Tales of the Sea. By J. A.
Barry. Author of 'Steve Brown's Bunyip.' *Crown 8vo. 6s.*

JAMES GORDON

THE VILLAGE AND THE DOCTOR. By James Gordon.
Crown 8vo. 6s.

BERTRAM MITFORD

THE SIGN OF THE SPIDER. By Bertram Mitford.
Crown 8vo. 3s. 6d.
A story of South Africa.

A. SHIELD

THE SQUIRE OF WANDALES. By A. Shield. *Crown 8vo.*
3s. 6d.

G. W. STEEVENS

MONOLOGUES OF THE DEAD. By G. W. Steevens.
Foolscap 8vo. 3s. 6d.
A series of Soliloquies in which famous men of antiquity—Julius Cæsar, Nero,
Alcibiades, etc., attempt to express themselves in the modes of thought and
language of to-day.

S. GORDON

A HANDFUL OF EXOTICS. By S. Gordon. *Crown 8vo.*
3s. 6d.
A volume of stories of Jewish life in Russia.

P. NEUMANN

THE SUPPLANTER. By P. Neumann. *Crown 8vo. 3s. 6d.*

EVELYN DICKINSON

THE SIN OF ANGELS. By Evelyn Dickinson. *Crown 8vo.*
3s. 6d.

H. A. KENNEDY

A MAN WITH BLACK EYELASHES. By H. A. Kennedy.
Crown 8vo. 3s. 6d.

MESSRS. METHUEN'S
PUBLICATIONS

───────◆───────

Poetry

Rudyard Kipling. BARRACK-ROOM BALLADS; And Other Verses. By RUDYARD KIPLING. *Ninth Edition. Crown 8vo. 6s.*

'Mr. Kipling's verse is strong, vivid, full of character. . . . Unmistakable genius rings in every line.'—*Times.*

'"Barrack-Room Ballads" contains some of the best work that Mr. Kipling has ever done, which is saying a good deal. "Fuzzy-Wuzzy," "Gunga Din," and "Tommy," are, in our opinion, altogether superior to anything of the kind that English literature has hitherto produced.'—*Athenæum.*

'The ballads teem with imagination, they palpitate with emotion. We read them with laughter and tears; the metres throb in our pulses, the cunningly ordered words tingle with life; and if this be not poetry, what is?'—*Pall Mall Gazette.*

"Q." THE GOLDEN POMP: A Procession of English Lyrics from Surrey to Shirley, arranged by A. T. QUILLER COUCH. *Crown 8vo. Buckram. 6s.*

'A delightful volume: a really golden "Pomp."'—*Spectator.*

"Q." GREEN BAYS: Verses and Parodies. By "Q.," Author of 'Dead Man's Rock,' etc. *Second Edition. Crown 8vo. 3s. 6d.*

'The verses display a rare and versatile gift of parody, great command of metre, and a very pretty turn of humour.'—*Times.*

H. C. Beeching. LYRA SACRA: An Anthology of Sacred Verse. Edited by H. C. BEECHING, M.A. *Crown 8vo. Buckram. 6s.*

'An anthology of high excellence.'—*Athenæum.*

'A charming selection, which maintains a lofty standard of excellence.'—*Times.*

W. B. Yeats. AN ANTHOLOGY OF IRISH VERSE. Edited by W. B. YEATS. *Crown 8vo. 3s. 6d.*

'An attractive and catholic selection.'—*Times.*

'It is edited by the most original and most accomplished of modern Irish poets, and against his editing but a single objection can be brought, namely, that it excludes from the collection his own delicate lyrics.'—*Saturday Review.*

E. Mackay. A SONG OF THE SEA: MY LADY OF DREAMS, AND OTHER POEMS. By ERIC MACKAY, Author of 'The Love Letters of a Violinist.' *Second Edition. Fcap. 8vo, gilt top. 5s.*

'Everywhere Mr. Mackay displays himself the master of a style marked by all the characteristics of the best rhetoric. He has a keen sense of rhythm and of general balance; his verse is excellently sonorous.'—*Globe.*

'Throughout the book the poetic workmanship is fine.'—*Scotsman.*

Ibsen. BRAND. A Drama by HENRIK IBSEN. Translated by
WILLIAM WILSON. *Second Edition. Crown 8vo. 3s. 6d.*

'The greatest world-poem of the nineteenth century next to "Faust." It is in
the same set with "Agamemnon," with "Lear," with the literature that we now
instinctively regard as high and holy.'—*Daily Chronicle.*

"A. G." VERSES TO ORDER. By "A. G." *Cr. 8vo. 2s. 6d.
net.*

A small volume of verse by a writer whose initials are well known to Oxford men.
'A capital specimen of light academic poetry. These verses are very bright and
engaging, easy and sufficiently witty.'—*St. James's Gazette.*

F. Langbridge. BALLADS OF THE BRAVE : Poems of
Chivalry, Enterprise, Courage, and Constancy, from the Earliest
Times to the Present Day. Edited, with Notes, by Rev. F. LANG-
BRIDGE. *Crown 8vo. Buckram. 3s. 6d. School Edition. 2s. 6d.*

'A very happy conception happily carried out. These "Ballads of the Brave" are
intended to suit the real tastes of boys, and will suit the taste of the great majority.'
—*Spectator.*   'The book is full of splendid things.'—*World.*

Lang and Craigie. THE POEMS OF ROBERT BURNS.
Edited by ANDREW LANG and W. A. CRAIGIE. With Portrait.
Demy 8vo, gilt top. 6s.

This edition contains a carefully collated Text, numerous Notes critical and textual,
a critical and biographical Introduction, and a Glossary.
'Among the editions in one volume, Mr. Andrew Lang's will take the place of
authority.'—*Times.*
'To the general public the beauty of its type, and the fair proportions of its pages, as
well as the excellent chronological arrangement of the poems, should make it
acceptable enough. Mr. Lang and his publishers have certainly succeeded in
producing an attractive popular edition of the poet, in which the brightly written
biographical introduction is not the least notable feature.'—*Glasgow Herald.*

English Classics

Edited by W. E. HENLEY.

'Very dainty volumes are these ; the paper, type, and light-green binding are all
very agreeable to the eye. *Simplex munditiis* is the phrase that might be applied
to them.'—*Globe.*
'The volumes are strongly bound in green buckram, are of a convenient size, and
pleasant to look upon, so that whether on the shelf, or on the table, or in the hand
the possessor is thoroughly content with them.'—*Guardian.*
'The paper, type, and binding of this edition are in excellent taste, and leave
nothing to be desired by lovers of literature.'—*Standard.*

THE LIFE AND OPINIONS OF TRISTRAM SHANDY.
By LAWRENCE STERNE. With an Introduction by CHARLES
WHIBLEY, and a Portrait. *2 vols. 7s.*

THE COMEDIES OF WILLIAM CONGREVE With
an Introduction by G. S. STREET, and a Portrait. *2 vols. 7s.*

THE ADVENTURES OF HAJJI BABA OF ISPAHAN. By JAMES MORIER. With an Introduction by E. G. BROWNE, M.A., and a Portrait. *2 vols. 7s.*

THE LIVES OF DONNE, WOTTON, HOOKER, HERBERT, AND SANDERSON. By IZAAK WALTON. With an Introduction by VERNON BLACKBURN, and a Portrait. *3s. 6d.*

THE LIVES OF THE ENGLISH POETS. By SAMUEL JOHNSON, LL.D. With an Introduction by J. H. MILLAR, and a Portrait. *3 vols. 10s. 6d.*

Illustrated Books

Jane Barlow. THE BATTLE OF THE FROGS AND MICE, translated by JANE BARLOW, Author of 'Irish Idylls,' and pictured by F. D. BEDFORD. *Small 4to. 6s. net.*

S. Baring Gould. A BOOK OF FAIRY TALES retold by S. BARING GOULD. With numerous illustrations and initial letters by ARTHUR J. GASKIN. *Second Edition. Crown 8vo. Buckram. 6s.*

'Mr. Baring Gould has done a good deed, and is deserving of gratitude, in re-writing in honest, simple style the old stories that delighted the childhood of " our fathers and grandfathers." We do not think he has omitted any of our favourite stories, the stories that are commonly regarded as merely " old fashioned." As to the form of the book, and the printing, which is by Messrs. Constable, it were difficult to commend overmuch. —*Saturday Review.*

S. Baring Gould. OLD ENGLISH FAIRY TALES. Collected and edited by S. BARING GOULD. With Numerous Illustrations by F. D. BEDFORD. *Second Edition. Crown 8vo. Buckram. 6s.*

' A charming volume, which children will be sure to appreciate. The stories have been selected with great ingenuity from various old ballads and folk-tales, and, having been somewhat altered and readjusted, now stand forth, clothed in Mr. Baring Gould's delightful English, to enchant youthful readers. All the tales are good.'—*Guardian.*

S. Baring Gould. A BOOK OF NURSERY SONGS AND RHYMES. Edited by S. BARING GOULD, and Illustrated by the Birmingham Art School. *Buckram, gilt top. Crown 8vo. 6s.*

' The volume is very complete in its way, as it contains nursery songs to the number of 77, game-rhymes, and jingles. To the student we commend the sensible introduction, and the explanatory notes. The volume is superbly printed on soft, thick paper, which it is a pleasure to touch ; and the borders and pictures are, as we have said, among the very best specimens we have seen of the Gaskin school.' —*Birmingham Gazette.*

H. C. Beeching. A BOOK OF CHRISTMAS VERSE. Edited by H. C. BEECHING, M.A., and Illustrated by WALTER CRANE. *Crown 8vo, gilt top.* 5s.

A collection of the best verse inspired by the birth of Christ from the Middle Ages to the present day. A distinction of the book is the large number of poems it contains by modern authors, a few of which are here printed for the first time.

'An anthology which, from its unity of aim and high poetic excellence, has a better right to exist than most of its fellows.'—*Guardian.*

History

Gibbon. THE DECLINE AND FALL OF THE ROMAN EMPIRE. By EDWARD GIBBON. A New Edition, Edited with Notes, Appendices, and Maps, by J. B. BURY, M.A., Fellow of Trinity College, Dublin. *In Seven Volumes. Demy 8vo. Gilt top.* 8s. 6d. each. *Also crown 8vo.* 6s. each. *Vol. I.*

'The time has certainly arrived for a new edition of Gibbon's great work. . . . Professor Bury is the right man to undertake this task. His learning is amazing, both in extent and accuracy. The book is issued in a handy form, and at a moderate price, and it is admirably printed.'—*Times.*

'The edition is edited as a classic should be edited, removing nothing, yet indicating the value of the text, and bringing it up to date. It promises to be of the utmost value, and will be a welcome addition to many libraries.'—*Scotsman.*

'This edition, so far as one may judge from the first instalment, is a marvel of erudition and critical skill, and it is the very minimum of praise to predict that the seven volumes of it will supersede Dean Milman's as the standard edition of our great historical classic.'—*Glasgow Herald.*

'The beau-ideal Gibbon has arrived at last.'—*Sketch.*

'At last there is an adequate modern edition of Gibbon. . . . The best edition the nineteenth century could produce.'—*Manchester Guardian.*

Flinders Petrie. A HISTORY OF EGYPT, FROM THE EARLIEST TIMES TO THE PRESENT DAY. Edited by W. M. FLINDERS PETRIE, D.C.L., LL.D., Professor of Egyptology at University College. *Fully Illustrated. In Six Volumes. Crown 8vo.* 6s. each.

Vol. I. PREHISTORIC TIMES TO XVI. DYNASTY. W. M. F. Petrie. *Second Edition.*

'A history written in the spirit of scientific precision so worthily represented by Dr. Petrie and his school cannot but promote sound and accurate study, and supply a vacant place in the English literature of Egyptology.'—*Times.*

Flinders Petrie. EGYPTIAN TALES. Edited by W. M. FLINDERS PETRIE. Illustrated by TRISTRAM ELLIS. *In Two Volumes. Crown 8vo.* 3s. 6d. each.

'A valuable addition to the literature of comparative folk-lore. The drawings are really illustrations in the literal sense of the word.'—*Globe.*

'It has a scientific value to the student of history and archæology.'—*Scotsman.*

'Invaluable as a picture of life in Palestine and Egypt.'—*Daily News.*

Flinders Petrie. EGYPTIAN DECORATIVE ART. By W. M. FLINDERS PETRIE, D.C.L. With 120 Illustrations. *Crown 8vo. 3s. 6d.*

'Professor Flinders Petrie is not only a profound Egyptologist, but an accomplished student of comparative archæology. In these lectures, delivered at the Royal Institution, he displays both qualifications with rare skill in elucidating the development of decorative art in Egypt, and in tracing its influence on the art of other countries. Few experts can speak with higher authority and wider knowledge than the Professor himself, and in any case his treatment of his subject is full of learning and insight.'—*Times.*

S. Baring Gould. THE TRAGEDY OF THE CÆSARS. The Emperors of the Julian and Claudian Lines. With numerous Illustrations from Busts, Gems, Cameos, etc. By S. BARING GOULD, Author of 'Mehalah,' etc. *Third Edition. Royal 8vo. 15s.*

' A most splendid and fascinating book on a subject of undying interest. The great feature of the book is the use the author has made of the existing portraits of the Caesars, and the admirable critical subtlety he has exhibited in dealing with this line of research. It is brilliantly written, and the illustrations are supplied on a scale of profuse magnificence.'—*Daily Chronicle.*

' The volumes will in no sense disappoint the general reader. Indeed, in their way, there is nothing in any sense so good in English. . . . Mr. Baring Gould has presented his narrative in such a way as not to make one dull page.'—*Athenæum.*

A. Clark. THE COLLEGES OF OXFORD : Their History, their Traditions. By Members of the University. Edited by A. CLARK, M.A., Fellow and Tutor of Lincoln College. *8vo. 12s. 6d.*

' A work which will certainly be appealed to for many years as the standard book on the Colleges of Oxford.'—*Athenæum.*

Perrens. THE HISTORY OF FLORENCE FROM 1434 TO 1492. By F. T. PERRENS. Translated by HANNAH LYNCH. *8vo. 12s. 6d.*

A history of Florence under the domination of Cosimo, Piero, and Lorenzo de Medicis.

' This is a standard book by an honest and intelligent historian, who has deserved well of all who are interested in Italian history.'—*Manchester Guardian.*

E. L. S. Horsburgh. THE CAMPAIGN OF WATERLOO. By E. L. S. HORSBURGH, B.A. *With Plans. Crown 8vo. 5s.*

' A brilliant essay—simple, sound, and thorough.'—*Daily Chronicle.*

' A study, the most concise, the most lucid, the most critical that has been produced.' —*Birmingham Mercury.*

' A careful and precise study, a fair and impartial criticism, and an eminently readable book.'—*Admiralty and Horse Guards Gazette.*

H. B. George. BATTLES OF ENGLISH HISTORY. By H. B. GEORGE, M.A., Fellow of New College, Oxford. *With numerous Plans. Third Edition. Crown 8vo. 6s.*

' Mr. George has undertaken a very useful task—that of making military affairs intelligible and instructive to non-military readers—and has executed it with laudable intelligence and industry, and with a large measure of success.'—*Times.*

' This book is almost a revelation ; and we heartily congratulate the author on his work and on the prospect of the reward he has well deserved for so much conscientious and sustained labour.'—*Daily Chronicle.*

O. Browning. A SHORT HISTORY OF MEDIÆVAL ITALY,
A.D. 1250-1530.   By OSCAR BROWNING, Fellow and Tutor of King's
College, Cambridge.   *Second Edition.   In Two Volumes.   Crown
8vo.   5s. each.*

> VOL. I. 1250-1409.—Guelphs and Ghibellines.
> VOL. II. 1409-1530.—The Age of the Condottieri.

'A vivid picture of mediæval Italy.'—*Standard.*
'Mr. Browning is to be congratulated on the production of a work of immense
labour and learning.'—*Westminster Gazette.*

O'Grady.   THE   STORY   OF   IRELAND.   By STANDISH
O'GRADY, Author of 'Finn and his Companions.'   *Cr. 8vo.   2s. 6d.*
'Most delightful, most stimulating.   Its racy humour, its original imaginings,
make it one of the freshest, breeziest volumes.'—*Methodist Times.*
'A survey at once graphic, acute, and quaintly written.'—*Times.*

Biography

R. L. Stevenson.   VAILIMA   LETTERS.   By ROBERT LOUIS
STEVENSON.   With an Etched Portrait by WILLIAM STRANG, and
other Illustrations.   *Second Edition.   Crown 8vo.   Buckram.   7s. 6d.*

'The Vailima Letters are rich in all the varieties of that charm which have secured
for Stevenson the affection of many others besides "journalists, fellow-novelists,
and boys."'—*The Times.*
'Few publications have in our time been more eagerly awaited than these "Vailima
Letters," giving the first fruits of the correspondence of Robert Louis Stevenson.
But, high as the tide of expectation has run, no reader can possibly be disappointed
in the result.'—*St. James's Gazette.*
'For the student of English literature these letters indeed are a treasure.   They
are more like "Scott's Journal" in kind than any other literary autobiography.'
—*National Observer.*

F. W. Joyce.   THE   LIFE   OF   SIR   FREDERICK   GORE
OUSELEY.   By F. W. JOYCE, M.A.   With Portraits and Illustrations.   *Crown 8vo.   7s. 6d.*

'All the materials have been well digested, and the book gives us a complete picture
of the life of one who will ever be held in loving remembrance by his personal
friends, and who in the history of music in this country will always occupy a
prominent position on account of the many services he rendered to the art.'—
Musical News.
'This book has been undertaken in quite the right spirit, and written with sympathy,
insight, and considerable literary skill.'—*Times.*

W. G. Collingwood.   THE LIFE OF JOHN RUSKIN.   By
W. G. COLLINGWOOD, M.A., Editor of Mr. Ruskin's Poems.   With
numerous Portraits, and 13 Drawings by Mr. Ruskin.   *Second
Edition.   2 vols.   8vo.   32s.*

'No more magnificent volumes have been published for a long time.'—*Times.*
'It is long since we had a biography with such delights of substance and of form.
Such a book is a pleasure for the day, and a joy for ever.'—*Daily Chronicle.*
'A noble monument of a noble subject.   One of the most beautiful books about one
of the noblest lives of our century.'—*Glasgow Herald.*

C. Waldstein. JOHN RUSKIN: a Study. By CHARLES WALDSTEIN, M.A., Fellow of King's College, Cambridge. With a Photogravure Portrait after Professor HERKOMER. *Post 8vo.* 5*s.*

'A thoughtful, impartial, well-written criticism of Ruskin's teaching, intended to separate what the author regards as valuable and permanent from what is transient and erroneous in the great master's writing.'—*Daily Chronicle.*

W. H. Hutton. THE LIFE OF SIR THOMAS MORE. By W. H. HUTTON, M.A., Author of 'William Laud.' *With Portraits. Crown 8vo.* 5*s.*

'The book lays good claim to high rank among our biographies. It is excellently, even lovingly, written.'—*Scotsman.*
'An excellent monograph.'—*Times.*
'A most complete presentation.'—*Daily Chronicle.*

M. Kaufmann. CHARLES KINGSLEY. By M. KAUFMANN, M.A. *Crown 8vo. Buckram.* 5*s.*

A biography of Kingsley, especially dealing with his achievements in social reform.
'The author has certainly gone about his work with conscientiousness and industry. — *Sheffield Daily Telegraph.*

A. F. Robbins. THE EARLY LIFE OF WILLIAM EWART GLADSTONE. By A. F. ROBBINS. *With Portraits. Crown 8vo.* 6*s.*

'Considerable labour and much skill of presentation have not been unworthily expended on this interesting work.'—*Times.*

Clark Russell. THE LIFE OF ADMIRAL LORD COLLINGWOOD. By W. CLARK RUSSELL, Author of 'The Wreck of the Grosvenor.' With Illustrations by F. BRANGWYN. *Third Edition. Crown 8vo.* 6*s.*

'A most excellent and wholesome book, which we should like to see in the hands of every boy in the country.'—*St. James's Gazette.*
'A really good book.'—*Saturday Review.*

Southey. ENGLISH SEAMEN (Howard, Clifford, Hawkins, Drake, Cavendish). By ROBERT SOUTHEY. Edited, with an Introduction, by DAVID HANNAY. *Second Edition. Crown 8vo.* 6*s.*

'Admirable and well-told stories of our naval history.'—*Army and Navy Gazette.*
'A brave, inspiriting book.'—*Black and White.*
'The work of a master of style, and delightful all through.'—*Daily Chronicle.*

General Literature

S. Baring Gould. OLD COUNTRY LIFE. By S. BARING GOULD, Author of 'Mehalah,' etc. With Sixty-seven Illustrations by W. PARKINSON, F. D. BEDFORD, and F. MASEY. *Large Crown 8vo.* 10*s.* 6*d. Fifth and Cheaper Edition.* 6*s.*

'"Old Country Life," as healthy wholesome reading, full of breezy life and movement, full of quaint stories vigorously told, will not be excelled by any book to be published throughout the year. Sound, hearty, and English to the core.'—*World.*

S. Baring Gould. HISTORIC ODDITIES AND STRANGE
EVENTS. By S. BARING GOULD. *Third Edition. Crown 8vo.* 6s.
'A collection of exciting and entertaining chapters. The whole volume is delightful
reading.'—*Times.*

S. Baring Gould. FREAKS OF FANATICISM. By S. BARING
GOULD. *Third Edition. Crown 8vo.* 6s.
'Mr. Baring Gould has a keen eye for colour and effect, and the subjects he has
chosen give ample scope to his descriptive and analytic faculties. A perfectly
fascinating book.'—*Scottish Leader.*

S. Baring Gould. A GARLAND OF COUNTRY SONG:
English Folk Songs with their Traditional Melodies. Collected and
arranged by S. BARING GOULD and H. FLEETWOOD SHEPPARD.
Demy 4to. 6s.

S. Baring Gould. SONGS OF THE WEST: Traditional
Ballads and Songs of the West of England, with their Traditional
Melodies. Collected by S. BARING GOULD, M.A., and H. FLEET-
WOOD SHEPPARD, M.A. Arranged for Voice and Piano. In 4 Parts
(containing 25 Songs each), *Parts I., II., III.,* 3s. *each. Part
IV.,* 5s. *In one Vol., French morocco,* 15s.
'A rich collection of humour, pathos, grace, and poetic fancy.'—*Saturday Review.*

S. Baring Gould. YORKSHIRE ODDITIES AND STRANGE
EVENTS. *Fourth Edition. Crown 8vo.* 6s.

S. Baring Gould. STRANGE SURVIVALS AND SUPER-
STITIONS. With Illustrations. By S. BARING GOULD. *Crown
8vo. Second Edition.* 6s.
'We have read Mr. Baring Gould's book from beginning to end. It is full of quaint
and various information, and there is not a dull page in it.'—*Notes and Queries.*

S. Baring Gould. THE DESERTS OF SOUTHERN
FRANCE. By S. BARING GOULD. With numerous Illustrations
by F. D. BEDFORD, S. HUTTON, etc. *2 vols. Demy 8vo.* 32s.
This book is the first serious attempt to describe the great barren tableland that
extends to the south of Limousin in the Department of Aveyron, Lot, etc., a
country of dolomite cliffs, and cañons, and subterranean rivers. The region is
full of prehistoric and historic interest, relics of cave-dwellers, of mediæval
robbers, and of the English domination and the Hundred Years' War.
'His two richly-illustrated volumes are full of matter of interest to the geologist,
the archæologist, and the student of history and manners.'—*Scotsman.*
'It deals with its subject in a manner which rarely fails to arrest attention.'—*Times.*

R. S. Baden-Powell. THE DOWNFALL OF PREMPEH. A
Diary of Life with the Native Levy in Ashanti, 1895. By Lieut.-Col.
BADEN-POWELL. With 21 Illustrations, a Map, and a Special
Chapter on the Political and Commercial Position of Ashanti by Sir
GEORGE BADEN-POWELL, K.C.M.G., M.P. *Demy 8vo.* 10s. 6d.
'A compact, faithful, most readable record of the campaign.'—*Daily News.*
'A bluff and vigorous narrative.'—*Glasgow Herald.*
'A really interesting book.'—*Yorkshire Post.*

W. E. Gladstone. THE SPEECHES AND PUBLIC ADDRESSES OF THE RT. HON. W. E. GLADSTONE, M.P. Edited by A. W. HUTTON, M.A., and H. J. COHEN, M.A. With Portraits. *8vo. Vols. IX. and X. 12s. 6d. each.*

Henley and Whibley. A BOOK OF ENGLISH PROSE. Collected by W. E. HENLEY and CHARLES WHIBLEY. *Cr. 8vo. 6s.*

'A unique volume of extracts—an art gallery of early prose.'—*Birmingham Post.*
'An admirable companion to Mr. Henley's "Lyra Heroica."'—*Saturday Review.*
'Quite delightful. The choice made has been excellent, and the volume has been most admirably printed by Messrs. Constable. A greater treat for those not well acquainted with pre-Restoration prose could not be imagined.'—*Athenæum.*

J. Wells. OXFORD AND OXFORD LIFE. By Members of the University. Edited by J. WELLS, M.A., Fellow and Tutor of Wadham College. *Crown 8vo. 3s. 6d.*

This work contains an account of life at Oxford—intellectual, social, and religious—a careful estimate of necessary expenses, a review of recent changes, a statement of the present position of the University, and chapters on Women's Education, aids to study, and University Extension.
'We congratulate Mr. Wells on the production of a readable and intelligent account of Oxford as it is at the present time, written by persons who are possessed of a close acquaintance with the system and life of the University.'—*Athenæum.*

W. M. Dixon. A PRIMER OF TENNYSON. By W. M. DIXON, M.A., Professor of English Literature at Mason College. *Crown 8vo. 2s. 6d.*

'Much sound and well-expressed criticism and acute literary judgments. The bibliography is a boon.'—*Speaker.*
'No better estimate of the late Laureate's work has yet been published. His sketch of Tennyson's life contains everything essential; his bibliography is full and concise: his literary criticism is most interesting.'—*Glasgow Herald.*

W. A. Craigie. A PRIMER OF BURNS. By W. A. CRAIGIE. *Crown 8vo. 2s. 6d.*

This book is planned on a method similar to the 'Primer of Tennyson.' It has also a glossary.
'A valuable addition to the literature of the poet.'—*Times.*
'An excellent short account.'—*Pall Mall Gazette.*
'An admirable introduction.'—*Globe.*

L. Whibley. GREEK OLIGARCHIES : THEIR ORGANISATION AND CHARACTER. By L. WHIBLEY, M.A., Fellow of Pembroke College, Cambridge. *Crown 8vo. 6s.*

'An exceedingly useful handbook : a careful and well-arranged study of an obscure subject.'—*Times.*
'Mr. Whibley is never tedious or pedantic.'—*Pall Mall Gazette.*

W. B. Worsfold. SOUTH AFRICA : Its History and its Future. By W. BASIL WORSFOLD, M.A. *With a Map. Crown 8vo. 6s.*

'An intensely interesting book.'—*Daily Chronicle.*
'A monumental work compressed into a very moderate compass.'—*World.*

A 3

C. H. Pearson. ESSAYS AND CRITICAL REVIEWS. By C. H. PEARSON, M.A., Author of 'National Life and Character.' Edited, with a Biographical Sketch, by H. A. STRONG, M.A., LL.D. With a Portrait. *Demy 8vo.* 10s. 6d.

'These fine essays illustrate the great breadth of his historical and literary sympathies and the remarkable variety of his intellectual interests.'—*Glasgow Herald.*
'Remarkable for careful handling, breadth of view, and thorough knowledge.'—*Scotsman.*
'Charming essays.'—*Spectator.*

Ouida. VIEWS AND OPINIONS. By OUIDA. *Crown 8vo. Second Edition.* 6s.

' Ouida is outspoken, and the reader of this book will not have a dull moment. The book is full of variety, and sparkles with entertaining matter.'—*Speaker.*

J. S. Shedlock. THE PIANOFORTE SONATA: Its Origin and Development. By J. S. SHEDLOCK. *Crown 8vo.* 5s.

' This work should be in the possession of every musician and amateur, for it not only embodies a concise and lucid history of the origin of one of the most important forms of musical composition, but, by reason of the painstaking research and accuracy of the author's statements, it is a very valuable work for reference.' —*Athenæum.*

E. M. Bowden. THE EXAMPLE OF BUDDHA: Being Quotations from Buddhist Literature for each Day in the Year. Compiled by E. M. BOWDEN. With Preface by Sir EDWIN ARNOLD. *Third Edition.* 16mo. 2s. 6d.

J. Beever. PRACTICAL FLY-FISHING, Founded on Nature, by JOHN BEEVER, late of the Thwaite House, Coniston. A New Edition, with a Memoir of the Author by W. G. COLLINGWOOD, M.A. *Crown 8vo.* 3s. 6d.

A little book on Fly-Fishing by an old friend of Mr. Ruskin.

Science

Freudenreich. DAIRY BACTERIOLOGY. A Short Manual for the Use of Students. By Dr. ED. VON FREUDENREICH. Translated from the German by J. R. AINSWORTH DAVIS, B.A., F.C.P. *Crown 8vo.* 2s. 6d.

Chalmers Mitchell. OUTLINES OF BIOLOGY. By P. CHALMERS MITCHELL, M.A., F.Z.S. *Fully Illustrated. Crown 8vo.* 6s.

A text-book designed to cover the new Schedule issued by the Royal College of Physicians and Surgeons.

G. Massee. A MONOGRAPH OF THE MYXOGASTRES. By GEORGE MASSEE. With 12 Coloured Plates. *Royal 8vo.* 18s. net.

' A work much in advance of any book in the language treating of this group of organisms. It is indispensable to every student of the Myxogastres. The coloured plates deserve high praise for their accuracy and execution.'—*Nature.*

Philosophy

L. T. Hobhouse. THE THEORY OF KNOWLEDGE. By L. T. HOBHOUSE, Fellow and Tutor of Corpus College, Oxford. *Demy 8vo.* 21*s.*

'The most important contribution to English philosophy since the publication of Mr. Bradley's "Appearance and Reality." Full of brilliant criticism and of positive theories which are models of lucid statement.'—*Glasgow Herald.*

'An elaborate and often brilliantly written volume. The treatment is one of great freshness, and the illustrations are particularly numerous and apt.'—*Times.*

W. H. Fairbrother. THE PHILOSOPHY OF T. H. GREEN. By W. H. FAIRBROTHER, M.A., Lecturer at Lincoln College, Oxford. *Crown 8vo.* 3*s.* 6*d.*

This volume is expository, not critical, and is intended for senior students at the Universities and others, as a statement of Green's teaching, and an introduction to the study of Idealist Philosophy.

'In every way an admirable book. As an introduction to the writings of perhaps the most remarkable speculative thinker whom England has produced in the present century, nothing could be better than Mr. Fairbrother's exposition and criticism.'—*Glasgow Herald.*

F. W. Bussell. THE SCHOOL OF PLATO : its Origin and its Revival under the Roman Empire. By F. W. BUSSELL, M.A., Fellow and Tutor of Brasenose College, Oxford. *Demy 8vo.* 10*s.* 6*d.*

'A highly valuable contribution to the history of ancient thought.'—*Glasgow Herald.*

'A clever and stimulating book, provocative of thought and deserving careful reading.' —*Manchester Guardian.*

F. S. Granger. THE WORSHIP OF THE ROMANS. By F. S. GRANGER, M.A., Litt.D., Professor of Philosophy at University College, Nottingham. *Crown 8vo.* 6*s.*

The author has attempted to delineate that group of beliefs which stood in close connection with the Roman religion, and, among the subjects treated are Dreams, Nature Worship, Roman Magic, Divination, Holy Places, Victims, etc. Thus the book is, apart from its immediate subject, a contribution to folk-lore and comparative psychology.

'A scholarly analysis of the religious ceremonies, beliefs, and superstitions of ancient Rome, conducted in the new instructive light of comparative anthropology.'— *Times.*

Theology

E. C. S. Gibson. THE XXXIX. ARTICLES OF THE CHURCH OF ENGLAND. Edited with an Introduction by E. C. S. GIBSON, D.D., Vicar of Leeds, late Principal of Wells Theological College. *In Two Volumes. Demy 8vo. 7s. 6d. each. Vol. I. Articles I.-VIII.*

'The tone maintained throughout is not that of the partial advocate, but the faithful exponent.'—*Scotsman.*

'There are ample proofs of clearness of expression, sobriety of judgment, and breadth of view. . . . The book will be welcome to all students of the subject, and its sound, definite, and loyal theology ought to be of great service.'—*National Observer.*

'So far from repelling the general reader, its orderly arrangement, lucid treatment, and felicity of diction invite and encourage his attention.'—*Yorkshire Post.*

R. L. Ottley. THE DOCTRINE OF THE INCARNATION. By R. L. OTTLEY, M.A., late fellow of Magdalen College, Oxon., Principal of Pusey House. *In Two Volumes. Demy 8vo.* 15s.

'Learned and reverent : lucid and well arranged.'—*Record.*

'Accurate, well ordered, and judicious.'—*National Observer.*

'A clear and remarkably full account of the main currents of speculation. Scholarly precision . . . genuine tolerance . . . intense interest in his subject—are Mr. Ottley's merits.'—*Guardian.*

S. R. Driver. SERMONS ON SUBJECTS CONNECTED WITH THE OLD TESTAMENT. By S. R. DRIVER, D.D., Canon of Christ Church, Regius Professor of Hebrew in the University of Oxford. *Crown 8vo.* 6s.

'A welcome companion to the author's famous ' Introduction.' No man can read these discourses without feeling that Dr. Driver is fully alive to the deeper teaching of the Old Testament.'—*Guardian.*

T. K. Cheyne. FOUNDERS OF OLD TESTAMENT CRITICISM : Biographical, Descriptive, and Critical Studies. By T. K. CHEYNE, D.D., Oriel Professor of the Interpretation of Holy Scripture at Oxford. *Large crown 8vo.* 7s. 6d.

This important book is a historical sketch of O. T. Criticism in the form of biographical studies from the days of Eichhorn to those of Driver and Robertson Smith. It is the only book of its kind in English.

'A very learned and instructive work.'—*Times.*

C. H. Prior. CAMBRIDGE SERMONS. Edited by C. H. PRIOR, M.A., Fellow and Tutor of Pembroke College. *Crown 8vo.* 6s.

A volume of sermons preached before the University of Cambridge by various preachers, including the Archbishop of Canterbury and Bishop Westcott.

'A representative collection. Bishop Westcott's is a noble sermon.'—*Guardian.*

H. C. Beeching. SERMONS TO SCHOOLBOYS. By H. C. BEECHING, M.A., Rector of Yattendon, Berks. With a Preface by Canon SCOTT HOLLAND. *Crown 8vo.* 2s. 6d.

Seven sermons preached before the boys of Bradfield College.

E. B. Layard. RELIGION IN BOYHOOD. Notes on the Religious Training of Boys. With a Preface by J. R. ILLINGWORTH. By E. B. LAYARD, M.A. 18mo. 1s.

Devotional Books.

With Full-page Illustrations. Fcap. 8vo. Buckram. 3s. 6d. Padded morocco, 5s.

THE IMITATION OF CHRIST. By THOMAS À KEMPIS. With an Introduction by DEAN FARRAR. Illustrated by C. M. GERE, and printed in black and red. *Second Edition.*

'Amongst all the innumerable English editions of the "Imitation," there can have been few which were prettier than this one, printed in strong and handsome type by Messrs. Constable, with all the glory of red initials, and the comfort of buckram binding.'—*Glasgow Herald.*

THE CHRISTIAN YEAR. By JOHN KEBLE. With an Introduction and Notes by W. LOCK, M.A., Sub-Warden of Keble College, Ireland Professor at Oxford, Author of the 'Life of John Keble.' Illustrated by R. ANNING BELL.

'The present edition is annotated with all the care and insight to be expected from Mr. Lock. The progress and circumstances of its composition are detailed in the Introduction. There is an interesting Appendix on the MSS. of the "Christian Year," and another giving the order in which the poems were written. A "Short Analysis of the Thought" is prefixed to each, and any difficulty in the text is explained in a note.—*Guardian.*

'The most acceptable edition of this ever-popular work.'—*Globe.*

Leaders of Religion

Edited by H. C. BEECHING, M.A. *With Portraits, crown 8vo.*

A series of short biographies of the most prominent leaders of religious life and thought of all ages and countries.

The following are ready—

3/6

CARDINAL NEWMAN. By R. H. HUTTON.

JOHN WESLEY. By J. H. OVERTON, M.A.

BISHOP WILBERFORCE. By G. W. DANIEL, M.A.

CARDINAL MANNING. By A. W. HUTTON, M.A.

CHARLES SIMEON. By H. C. G. MOULE, M.A.

JOHN KEBLE. By WALTER LOCK, M.A.

THOMAS CHALMERS. By Mrs. OLIPHANT.

LANCELOT ANDREWES. By R. L. OTTLEY, M.A.

AUGUSTINE OF CANTERBURY. By E. L. Cutts, D.D.

WILLIAM LAUD. By W. H. Hutton, M.A.

JOHN KNOX. By F. M'Cunn.

JOHN HOWE. By R. F. Horton, D.D.

BISHOP KEN. By F. A. Clarke, M.A.

GEORGE FOX, THE QUAKER. By T. Hodgkin, D.C.L.

Other volumes will be announced in due course.

Fiction

SIX SHILLING NOVELS

Marie Corelli's Novels

Crown 8vo. 6s. each.

A ROMANCE OF TWO WORLDS. *Fourteenth Edition.*

VENDETTA. *Eleventh Edition.*

THELMA. *Fourteenth Edition.*

ARDATH. *Tenth Edition.*

THE SOUL OF LILITH. *Ninth Edition.*

WORMWOOD. *Eighth Edition.*

BARABBAS : A DREAM OF THE WORLD'S TRAGEDY.
Twenty-fifth Edition.

The tender reverence of the treatment and the imaginative beauty of the writing have reconciled us as to the daring of the conception, and the conviction is forced on us that even so exalted a subject cannot be made too familiar to us, provided it be presented in the true spirit of Christian faith. The amplifications of the Scripture narrative are often conceived with high poetic insight, and this "Dream of the World's Tragedy" is, despite some trifling incongruities, a lofty and not inadequate paraphrase of the supreme climax of the inspired narrative.'—*Dublin Review.*

THE SORROWS OF SATAN. *Twenty-ninth Edition.*

A very powerful piece of work. . . . The conception is magnificent, and is likely to win an abiding place within the memory of man. . . . The author has immense command of language, and a limitless audacity. . . . This interesting and remarkable romance will live long after much of the ephemeral literature of the day is forgotten. . . . A literary phenomenon . . novel, and even sublime.'—W. T. Stead in the *Review of Reviews.*

Anthony Hope's Novels

Crown 8vo.   6s. each.

THE GOD IN THE CAR.   *Seventh Edition.*

'A very remarkable book, deserving of critical analysis impossible within our limit; brilliant, but not superficial; well considered, but not elaborated; constructed with the proverbial art that conceals, but yet allows itself to be enjoyed by readers to whom fine literary method is a keen pleasure; true without cynicism, subtle without affectation, humorous without strain, witty without offence, inevitably sad, with an unmorose simplicity.'— *The World.*

A CHANGE OF AIR.   *Fourth Edition.*

'A graceful, vivacious comedy, true to human nature.   The characters are traced with a masterly hand.'—*Times.*

A MAN OF MARK.   *Third Edition.*

'Of all Mr. Hope's books, "A Man of Mark" is the one which best compares with "The Prisoner of Zenda."   The two romances are unmistakably the work of the same writer, and he possesses a style of narrative peculiarly seductive, piquant, comprehensive, and—his own.'—*National Observer.*

THE CHRONICLES OF COUNT ANTONIO.   *Third Edition.*

'It is a perfectly enchanting story of love and chivalry, and pure romance.   The outlawed Count is the most constant, desperate, and withal modest and tender of lovers, a peerless gentleman, an intrepid fighter, a very faithful friend, and a most magnanimous foe.   In short, he is an altogether admirable, lovable, and delightful hero.   There is not a word in the volume that can give offence to the most fastidious taste of man or woman, and there is not, either, a dull paragraph in it. The book is everywhere instinct with the most exhilarating spirit of adventure, and delicately perfumed with the sentiment of all heroic and honourable deeds of history and romance.'—*Guardian.*

S. Baring Gould's Novels

Crown 8vo.   6s. each.

'To say that a book is by the author of "Mehalah" is to imply that it contains a story cast on strong lines, containing dramatic possibilities, vivid and sympathetic descriptions of Nature, and a wealth of ingenious imagery.'—*Speaker.*

'That whatever Mr. Baring Gould writes is well worth reading, is a conclusion that may be very generally accepted.   His views of life are fresh and vigorous, his language pointed and characteristic, the incidents of which he makes use are striking and original, his characters are life-like, and though somewhat exceptional people, are drawn and coloured with artistic force.   Add to this that his descriptions of scenes and scenery are painted with the loving eyes and skilled hands of a master of his art, that he is always fresh and never dull, and under such conditions it is no wonder that readers have gained confidence both in his power of amusing and satisfying them, and that year by year his popularity widens.'—*Court Circular.*

ARMINELL : A Social Romance.   *Fourth Edition.*

URITH : A Story of Dartmoor.   *Fourth Edition.*

'The author is at his best.'—*Times.*
'He has nearly reached the high water-mark of "Mehalah." '—*National Observer.*

IN THE ROAR OF THE SEA. *Fifth Edition.*

'One of the best imagined and most enthralling stories the author has produced.
—*Saturday Review.*

MRS. CURGENVEN OF CURGENVEN. *Fourth Edition.*

' A novel of vigorous humour and sustained power.'—*Graphic.*
' The swing of the narrative is splendid.'—*Sussex Daily News.*

CHEAP JACK ZITA. *Third Edition.*

' A powerful drama of human passion.'—*Westminster Gazette.*
' A story worthy the author.'—*National Observer.*

THE QUEEN OF LOVE. *Fourth Edition.*

' The scenery is admirable, and the dramatic incidents are most striking.'—*Glasgow Herald.*
' Strong, interesting, and clever.'—*Westminster Gazette.*
' You cannot put it down until you have finished it.'—*Punch.*
' Can be heartily recommended to all who care for cleanly, energetic, and interesting fiction.'—*Sussex Daily News.*

KITTY ALONE. *Fourth Edition.*

' A strong and original story, teeming with graphic description, stirring incident, and, above all, with vivid and enthralling human interest.'—*Daily Telegraph.*
' Brisk, clever, keen, healthy, humorous, and interesting.'—*National Observer.*
' Full of quaint and delightful studies of character.'—*Bristol Mercury.*

NOÉMI : A Romance of the Cave-Dwellers. Illustrated by R. CATON WOODVILLE. *Third Edition.*

" Noémi " is as excellent a tale of fighting and adventure as one may wish to meet. All the characters that interfere in this exciting tale are marked with properties of their own. The narrative also runs clear and sharp as the Loire itself.'—*Pall Mall Gazette.*
' Mr. Baring Gould's powerful story is full of the strong lights and shadows and vivid colouring to which he has accustomed us.'—*Standard.*

THE BROOM-SQUIRE. Illustrated by FRANK DADD. *Third Edition.*

' A strain of tenderness is woven through the web of his tragic tale, and its atmosphere is sweetened by the nobility and sweetness of the heroine's character.'—*Daily News.*
' A story of exceptional interest that seems to us to be better than anything he has written of late.'—*Speaker.*   ' A powerful and striking story.'—*Guardian.*
' A powerful piece of work.'—*Black and White.*

Gilbert Parker's Novels

Crown 8vo.   6s. each.

PIERRE AND HIS PEOPLE. *Third Edition.*

'Stories happily conceived and finely executed. There is strength and genius in Mr. Parker's style.'—*Daily Telegraph.*

MRS. FALCHION. *Third Edition.*

'A splendid study of character.'—*Athenæum.*
'But little behind anything that has been done by any writer of our time.'—*Pall Mall Gazette.*
'A very striking and admirable novel.'—*St. James's Gazette.*

THE TRANSLATION OF A SAVAGE.

'The plot is original and one difficult to work out; but Mr. Parker has done it with great skill and delicacy. The reader who is not interested in this original, fresh, and well-told tale must be a dull person indeed.'—*Daily Chronicle.*
'A strong and successful piece of workmanship. The portrait of Lali, strong, dignified, and pure, is exceptionally well drawn.'—*Manchester Guardian.*

THE TRAIL OF THE SWORD. *Fourth Edition.*

'Everybody with a soul for romance will thoroughly enjoy "The Trail of the Sword."'—*St. James's Gazette.*
'A rousing and dramatic tale. A book like this, in which swords flash, great surprises are undertaken, and daring deeds done, in which men and women live and love in the old straightforward passionate way, is a joy inexpressible to the reviewer, brain-weary of the domestic tragedies and psychological puzzles of everyday fiction; and we cannot but believe that to the reader it will bring refreshment as welcome and as keen.'—*Daily Chronicle.*

WHEN VALMOND CAME TO PONTIAC: The Story of a Lost Napoleon. *Third Edition.*

'Here we find romance—real, breathing, living romance, but it runs flush with our own times, level with our own feelings. Not here can we complain of lack of inevitableness or homogeneity. The character of Valmond is drawn unerringly; his career, brief as it is, is placed before us as convincingly as history itself. The book must be read, we may say re-read, for any one thoroughly to appreciate Mr. Parker's delicate touch and innate sympathy with humanity.'—*Pall Mall Gazette.*
'The one work of genius which 1895 has as yet produced.'—*New Age.*

AN ADVENTURER OF THE NORTH: The Last Adventures of 'Pretty Pierre.'

'The present book is full of fine and moving stories of the great North, and it will add to Mr. Parker's already high reputation.'—*Glasgow Herald.*
'The new book is very romantic and very entertaining—full of that peculiarly elegant spirit of adventure which is so characteristic of Mr. Parker, and of that poetic thrill which has given him warmer, if less numerous, admirers than even his romantic story-telling gift has done.'—*Sketch.*

THE SEATS OF THE MIGHTY. *Illustrated. Fourth Edition.*

'The best thing he has done; one of the best things that any one has done lately.'—*St. James's Gazette.*
'Mr. Parker seems to become stronger and easier with every serious novel that he attempts. ... In "The Seats of the Mighty" he shows the matured power which his former novels have led us to expect, and has produced a really fine historical novel. ... The great creation of the book is Doltaire. ... His character is drawn with quite masterly strokes, for he is a villain who is not altogether a villain, and who attracts the reader, as he did the other characters, by the extraordinary brilliance of his gifts, and by the almost unconscious acts of nobility which he performs. ... Most sincerely is Mr. Parker to be congratulated on the finest novel he has yet written.'—*Athenæum.*

'Mr. Parker's latest book places him in the front rank of living novelists. "The Seats of the Mighty" is a great book.'—*Black and White.*

'One of the strongest stories of historical interest and adventure that we have read for many a day. . . . Through all Mr. Parker moves with an assured step, whilst in his treatment of his subject there is that happy blending of the poetical with the prosaic which has characterised all his writings. A notable and successful book.' —*Speaker.*

'The story is very finely and dramatically told. . . . In none of his books has his imaginative faculty appeared to such splendid purpose as here. Captain Moray, Alixe, Gabord, Vauban—above all, Doltaire—and, indeed, every person who takes part in the action of the story are clearly conceived and finely drawn and individualised.—*Scotsman.*

'An admirable romance. The glory of a romance is its plot, and this plot is crowded with fine sensations, which have no rest until the fall of the famous old city and the final restitution of love.'—*Pall Mall Gazette.*

Conan Doyle. ROUND THE RED LAMP. By A. CONAN DOYLE, Author of 'The White Company,' 'The Adventures of Sherlock Holmes,' etc. *Fourth Edition. Crown 8vo. 6s.*

'The book is, indeed, composed of leaves from life, and is far and away the best view that has been vouchsafed us behind the scenes of the consulting-room. It is very superior to "The Diary of a late Physician."'—*Illustrated London News.*

Stanley Weyman. UNDER THE RED ROBE. By STANLEY WEYMAN, Author of 'A Gentleman of France.' With Twelve Illustrations by R. Caton Woodville. *Eighth Edition. Crown 8vo. 6s.*

'A book of which we have read every word for the sheer pleasure of reading, and which we put down with a pang that we cannot forget it all and start again.'— *Westminster Gazette.*

'Every one who reads books at all must read this thrilling romance, from the first page of which to the last the breathless reader is haled along. An inspiration of "manliness and courage."—*Daily Chronicle.*

'A delightful tale of chivalry and adventure, vivid and dramatic, with a wholesome modesty and reverence for the highest.'—*Globe.*

Mrs. Clifford. A FLASH OF SUMMER. By MRS. W. K. CLIFFORD, Author of 'Aunt Anne,' etc. *Second Edition. Crown 8vo. 6s.*

'The story is a very sad and a very beautiful one, exquisitely told, and enriched with many subtle touches of wise and tender insight. It will, undoubtedly, add to its author's reputation—already high—in the ranks of novelists.'—*Speaker.*

'We must congratulate Mrs. Clifford upon a very successful and interesting story, told throughout with finish and a delicate sense of proportion, qualities which, indeed, have always distinguished the best work of this very able writer.'— *Manchester Guardian.*

Emily Lawless. HURRISH. By the Honble. EMILY LAWLESS, Author of 'Maelcho,' etc. *Fifth Edition. Crown 8vo. 6s.*
A reissue of Miss Lawless' most popular novel, uniform with 'Maelcho.'

Emily Lawless. MAELCHO : a Sixteenth Century Romance. By the Honble. EMILY LAWLESS, Author of 'Grania,' 'Hurrish,' etc. *Second Edition. Crown 8vo. 6s.*

'A really great book.'—*Spectator.*

'There is no keener pleasure in life than the recognition of genius. Good work is commoner than it used to be, but the best is as rare as ever. All the more gladly, therefore, do we welcome in "Maelcho" a piece of work of the first order, which we do not hesitate to describe as one of the most remarkable literary achievements of this generation. Miss Lawless is possessed of the very essence of historical genius.'—*Manchester Guardian.*

J. H. Findlater. THE GREEN GRAVES OF BALGOWRIE. By Jane H. Findlater. *Third Edition. Crown 8vo. 6s.*

'A powerful and vivid story.'—*Standard.*
'A beautiful story, sad and strange as truth itself.'—*Vanity Fair.*
'A work of remarkable interest and originality.'—*National Observer.*
'A really original novel.'—*Journal of Education.*
'A very charming and pathetic tale.'—*Pall Mall Gazette.*
'A singularly original, clever, and beautiful story.'—*Guardian.*
'"The Green Graves of Balgowrie" reveals to us a new Scotch writer of undoubted faculty and reserve force.'—*Spectator.*
'An exquisite idyll, delicate, affecting, and beautiful.'—*Black and White.*
'Permeated with high and noble purpose. It is one of the most wholesome stories we have met with, and cannot fail to leave a deep and lasting impression.'—*Newsagent.*

E. F. Benson. DODO: A DETAIL OF THE DAY. By E. F. Benson. *Sixteenth Edition. Crown 8vo. 6s.*

'A delightfully witty sketch of society.'—*Spectator.*
'A perpetual feast of epigram and paradox.'—*Speaker.*
'By a writer of quite exceptional ability.'—*Athenæum.*
'Brilliantly written.'—*World.*

E. F. Benson. THE RUBICON. By E. F. Benson, Author of 'Dodo.' *Fifth Edition. Crown 8vo. 6s.*

'Well written, stimulating, unconventional, and, in a word, characteristic.'—*Birmingham Post.*
'An exceptional achievement ; a notable advance on his previous work.'—*National Observer.*

M. M. Dowie. GALLIA. By Ménie Muriel Dowie, Author of 'A Girl in the Carpathians.' *Third Edition. Crown 8vo. 6s.*

'The style is generally admirable, the dialogue not seldom brilliant, the situations surprising in their freshness and originality, while the subsidiary as well as the principal characters live and move, and the story itself is readable from title-page to colophon.'—*Saturday Review.*
'A very notable book; a very sympathetically, at times delightfully written book. —*Daily Graphic.*

Mrs. Oliphant. SIR ROBERT'S FORTUNE. By Mrs. Oliphant. *Crown 8vo. 6s.*

'Full of her own peculiar charm of style and simple, subtle character-painting comes her new gift, the delightful story before us. The scene mostly lies in the moors, and at the touch of the authoress a Scotch moor becomes a living thing, strong, tender, beautiful, and changeful.'—*Pall Mall Gazette.*

Mrs. Oliphant. THE TWO MARYS. By Mrs. Oliphant. *Second Edition. Crown 8vo. 6s.*

W. E. Norris. MATTHEW AUSTIN. By W. E. Norris, Author of 'Mademoiselle de Mersac,' etc. *Fourth Edition. Crown 8vo. 6s.*

'"Matthew Austin" may safely be pronounced one of the most intellectually satisfactory and morally bracing novels of the current year.'—*Daily Telegraph.*

W. E. Norris. HIS GRACE. By W. E. Norris. *Third Edition. Crown 8vo. 6s.*

'Mr. Norris has drawn a really fine character in the Duke of Hurstbourne, at once unconventional and very true to the conventionalities of life, weak and strong in a breath, capable of inane follies and heroic decisions, yet not so definitely portrayed as to relieve a reader of the necessity of study.'—*Athenæum.*

W. E. Norris. THE DESPOTIC LADY AND OTHERS.
By W. E. NORRIS. *Crown 8vo.* 6s.

'A budget of good fiction of which no one will tire.'—*Scotsman.*
'An extremely entertaining volume—the sprightliest of holiday companions.'—*Daily Telegraph.*

H. G. Wells. THE STOLEN BACILLUS, and other Stories.
By H. G. WELLS, Author of 'The Time Machine.' *Crown
8vo.* 6s.

'The ordinary reader of fiction may be glad to know that these stories are eminently
readable from one cover to the other, but they are more than that ; they are the
impressions of a very striking imagination, which, it would seem, has a great deal
within its reach.'—*Saturday Review.*

Arthur Morrison. TALES OF MEAN STREETS. By ARTHUR
MORRISON. *Fourth Edition. Crown 8vo.* 6s.

'Told with consummate art and extraordinary detail. He tells a plain, unvarnished
tale, and the very truth of it makes for beauty. In the true humanity of the book
lies its justification, the permanence of its interest, and its indubitable triumph.'—
Athenæum.
'A great book. The author's method is amazingly effective, and produces a thrilling
sense of reality. The writer lays upon us a master hand. The book is simply
appalling and irresistible in its interest. It is humorous also ; without humour
it would not make the mark it is certain to make.'—*World.*

J. Maclaren Cobban. THE KING OF ANDAMAN : A
Saviour of Society. By J. MACLAREN COBBAN, Author of 'The
Red Sultan,' etc. *Crown 8vo.* 6s.

'An unquestionably interesting book. It would not surprise us if it turns out to be
the most interesting novel of the season, for it contains one character, at least,
who has in him the root of immortality, and the book itself is ever exhaling the
sweet savour of the unexpected. . . . Plot is forgotten and incident fades, and
only the really human endures, and throughout this book there stands out in bold
and beautiful relief its high-souled and chivalric protagonist, James the Master
of Hutcheon, the King of Andaman himself.'—*Pall Mall Gazette.*
'A most original and refreshing story. James Hutcheon is a personage whom it is
good to know and impossible to forget. He is beautiful within and without,
whichever way we take him.'—*Spectator.*
'"The King of Andaman," is a book which does credit not less to the heart than
the head of its author.'—*Athenæum.*
'The fact that Her Majesty the Queen has been pleased to gracefully express to the
author of "The King of Andaman" her interest in his work will doubtless find
for it many readers.'—*Vanity Fair.*

H. Morrah. A SERIOUS COMEDY. By HERBERT MORRAH.
Crown 8vo. 6s.

'There are many delightful places in this volume, which is well worthy of its title.
The theme has seldom been presented with more freshness or more force.'—
Scotsman.

L. B. Walford. SUCCESSORS TO THE TITLE. By MRS.
WALFORD, Author of 'Mr. Smith,' etc. *Second Edition. Crown
8vo.* 6s.

'The story is fresh and healthy from beginning to finish; and our liking for the two
simple people who are the successors to the title mounts steadily, and ends almost
in respect.'—*Scotsman.*
'The book is quite worthy to be ranked with many clever predecessors. It is excellent reading.'—*Glasgow Herald.*

T. L. Paton. A HOME IN INVERESK. By T. L. PATON. *Crown 8vo.* 6s.

'A distinctly fresh and fascinating novel.'—*Montrose Standard.*
'A book which bears marks of considerable promise.'—*Scotsman.*
'A pleasant and well-written story.'—*Daily Chronicle.*

John Davidson. MISS ARMSTRONG'S AND OTHER CIR-CUMSTANCES. By JOHN DAVIDSON. *Crown 8vo.* 6s.

''Throughout the volume there is a strong vein of originality, a strength in the handling, and a knowledge of human nature that are worthy of the highest praise.'
—*Scotsman.*

J. B. Burton. IN THE DAY OF ADVERSITY. By J. BLOUNDELLE BURTON, Author of 'The Hispaniola Plate,' etc. *Crown 8vo.* 6s.

'Unusually interesting and full of highly dramatic situations.'—*Guardian.*
'A well-written story, drawn from that inexhaustible mine, the time of Louis XIV.'
—*Pall Mall Gazette.*

H. Johnston. DR. CONGALTON'S LEGACY. By HENRY JOHNSTON. *Crown 8vo.* 6s.

'The story is redolent of humour, pathos, and tenderness, while it is not without a touch of tragedy.'—*Scotsman.*
'A worthy and permanent contribution to Scottish creative literature.'—*Glasgow Herald.*

Julian Corbett. A BUSINESS IN GREAT WATERS. By JULIAN CORBETT, Author of 'For God and Gold,' 'Kophetua XIIIth.,' etc. *Crown 8vo.* 6s.

'In this stirring story Mr. Julian Corbett has done excellent work, welcome alike for its distinctly literary flavour, and for the wholesome tone which pervades it. Mr. Corbett writes with immense spirit, and the book is a thoroughly enjoyable one in all respects. The salt of the ocean is in it, and the right heroic ring re-sounds through its gallant adventures.'—*Speaker.*

C. Phillips Woolley. THE QUEENSBERRY CUP. A Tale of Adventure. By CLIVE PHILLIPS WOOLLEY, Author of 'Snap,' Editor of 'Big Game Shooting.' *Illustrated. Crown 8vo.* 6s.

'A book which will delight boys: a book which upholds the healthy schoolboy code of morality.'—*Scotsman.*
'A brilliant book. Dick St. Clair, of Caithness, is an almost ideal character—a com-bination of the mediæval knight and the modern pugilist.'—*Admiralty and Horse-guards Gazette.*

Robert Barr. IN THE MIDST OF ALARMS. By ROBERT BARR, Author of 'From Whose Bourne,' etc. *Third Edition. Crown 8vo.* 6s.

'A book which has abundantly satisfied us by its capital humour.'—*Daily Chronicle.*
'Mr. Barr has achieved a triumph whereof he has every reason to be proud.'—*Pall Mall Gazette.*

L. Daintrey. THE KING OF ALBERIA. A Romance of the Balkans. By LAURA DAINTREY. *Crown 8vo.* 6s.

'Miss Daintrey seems to have an intimate acquaintance with the people and politics of the Balkan countries in which the scene of her lively and picturesque romance is laid. On almost every page we find clever touches of local colour which dif-ferentiate her book unmistakably from the ordinary novel of commerce. The story is briskly told, and well conceived.'—*Glasgow Herald.*

Mrs. Pinsent. CHILDREN OF THIS WORLD. By ELLEN F. PINSENT, Author of 'Jenny's Case.' *Crown 8vo.* 6s.
'Mrs. Pinsent's new novel has plenty of vigour, variety, and good writing. There are certainty of purpose, strength of touch, and clearness of vision.'—*Athenæum.*

Clark Russell. MY DANISH SWEETHEART. By W. CLARK RUSSELL, Author of 'The Wreck of the Grosvenor,' etc. *Illustrated. Fourth Edition. Crown 8vo.* 6s.

G. Manville Fenn. AN ELECTRIC SPARK. By G. MANVILLE FENN, Author of 'The Vicar's Wife,' 'A Double Knot,' etc. *Second Edition. Crown 8vo.* 6s.
'A simple and wholesome story.'—*Manchester Guardian.*

R. Pryce. TIME AND THE WOMAN. By RICHARD PRYCE, Author of 'Miss Maxwell's Affections,' 'The Quiet Mrs. Fleming,' etc. *Second Edition. Crown 8vo.* 6s.
'Mr. Pryce's work recalls the style of Octave Feuillet, by its clearness, conciseness, its literary reserve.'—*Athenæum.*

Mrs. Watson. THIS MAN'S DOMINION. By the Author of 'A High Little World.' *Second Edition. Crown 8vo.* 6s.

Marriott Watson. DIOGENES OF LONDON and other Sketches. By H. B. MARRIOTT WATSON, Author of 'The Web of the Spider.' *Crown 8vo. Buckram.* 6s.
'By all those who delight in the uses of words, who rate the exercise of prose above the exercise of verse, who rejoice in all proofs of its delicacy and its strength, who believe that English prose is chief among the moulds of thought, by these Mr. Marriott Watson's book will be welcomed.'—*National Observer.*

M. Gilchrist. THE STONE DRAGON. By MURRAY GILCHRIST. *Crown 8vo. Buckram.* 6s.
'The author's faults are atoned for by certain positive and admirable merits. The romances have not their counterpart in modern literature, and to read them is a unique experience.'—*National Observer.*

E. Dickinson. A VICAR'S WIFE. By EVELYN DICKINSON. *Crown 8vo.* 6s.

E. M. Gray. ELSA. By E. M'QUEEN GRAY. *Crown 8vo.* 6s.

THREE-AND-SIXPENNY NOVELS 3/6
Crown 8vo.

DERRICK VAUGHAN, NOVELIST. By EDNA LYALL.
MARGERY OF QUETHER. By S. BARING GOULD.
JACQUETTA. By S. BARING GOULD.
SUBJECT TO VANITY. By MARGARET BENSON.
THE MOVING FINGER. By MARY GAUNT.
JACO TRELOAR. By J. H. PEARCE.

AUT DIABOLUS AUT NIHIL. By X. L.

THE COMING OF CUCULAIN. A Romance of the Heroic
Age of Ireland. By STANDISH O'GRADY. *Illustrated.*

THE GODS GIVE MY DONKEY WINGS. By ANGUS
EVAN ABBOTT.

THE STAR GAZERS. By G. MANVILLE FENN.

THE POISON OF ASPS. By R. ORTON PROWSE.

THE QUIET MRS. FLEMING. By R. PRYCE.

THE PLAN OF CAMPAIGN. By F. MABEL ROBINSON.

DISENCHANTMENT. By F. MABEL ROBINSON.

MR. BUTLER'S WARD. By F. MABEL ROBINSON.

A LOST ILLUSION. By LESLIE KEITH.

A REVEREND GENTLEMAN. By J. M. COBBAN.

A DEPLORABLE AFFAIR. By W. E. NORRIS.

A CAVALIER'S LADYE. By Mrs. DICKER.

HALF-CROWN NOVELS
A Series of Novels by popular Authors.

2/6

1. HOVENDEN, V.C. By F. MABEL ROBINSON.
2. ELI'S CHILDREN. By G. MANVILLE FENN.
3. A DOUBLE KNOT. By G. MANVILLE FENN.
4. DISARMED. By M. BETHAM EDWARDS.
5. A MARRIAGE AT SEA. By W. CLARK RUSSELL.
6. IN TENT AND BUNGALOW. By the Author of 'Indian Idylls.'
7. MY STEWARDSHIP. By E. M'QUEEN GRAY.
8. JACK'S FATHER. By W. E. NORRIS.
9. JIM B.

Lynn Linton. THE TRUE HISTORY OF JOSHUA DAVID-
SON, Christian and Communist. By E. LYNN LINTON. *Eleventh
Edition. Post 8vo. 1s.*

Books for Boys and Girls 3/6
A Series of Books by well-known Authors, well illustrated.

1. THE ICELANDER'S SWORD. By S. BARING GOULD.
2. TWO LITTLE CHILDREN AND CHING. By EDITH
E. CUTHELL.

3. TODDLEBEN'S HERO. By M. M. BLAKE.
4. ONLY A GUARD ROOM DOG. By EDITH E. CUTHELL.
5. THE DOCTOR OF THE JULIET. By HARRY COLLING-
   WOOD.
6. MASTER ROCKAFELLAR'S VOYAGE. By W. CLARK
   RUSSELL.
7. SYD BELTON : Or, The Boy who would not go to Sea.
   By G. MANVILLE FENN.

The Peacock Library

*A Series of Books for Girls by well-known Authors,
handsomely bound in blue and silver, and well illustrated.*   **3/6**

1. A PINCH OF EXPERIENCE. By L. B. WALFORD.
2. THE RED GRANGE. By Mrs. MOLESWORTH.
3. THE SECRET OF MADAME DE MONLUC. By the
   Author of ' Mdle Mori.'
4. DUMPS. By Mrs. PARR, Author of 'Adam and Eve.'
5. OUT OF THE FASHION. By L. T. MEADE.
6. A GIRL OF THE PEOPLE. By L. T. MEADE.
7. HEPSY GIPSY. By L. T. MEADE. 2s. 6d.
8. THE HONOURABLE MISS. By L. T. MEADE.
9. MY LAND OF BEULAH. By Mrs. LEITH ADAMS.

University Extension Series

A series of books on historical, literary, and scientific subjects, suitable
for extension students and home-reading circles.   Each volume is complete in itself, and the subjects are treated by competent writers in a
broad and philosophic spirit.

Edited by J. E. SYMES, M.A.,

Principal of University College, Nottingham.

Crown 8vo.   Price (with some exceptions) 2s. 6d.

The following volumes are ready :—

THE INDUSTRIAL HISTORY OF ENGLAND. By H. DE
   B. GIBBINS, M.A., late Scholar of Wadham College, Oxon., Cobden
   Prizeman. *Fourth Edition.   With Maps and Plans.* 3s.

'A compact and clear story of our ndustrial development.   A study of this concise
   but luminous book cannot fail to give the reader a clear insight into the principal
   phenomena of our industrial history.   The editor and publishers are to be congratulated on this first volume of their venture, and we shall look with expectant
   interest for the succeeding volumes of the series.'—*University Extension Journal.*

A HISTORY OF ENGLISH POLITICAL ECONOMY. By L. L. PRICE, M.A., Fellow of Oriel College, Oxon. *Second Edition.*

PROBLEMS OF POVERTY: An Inquiry into the Industrial Conditions of the Poor. By J. A. HOBSON, M.A. *Third Edition.*

VICTORIAN POETS. By A. SHARP.

THE FRENCH REVOLUTION. By J. E. SYMES, M.A.

PSYCHOLOGY. By F. S. GRANGER, M.A., Lecturer in Philosophy at University College, Nottingham.

THE EVOLUTION OF PLANT LIFE: Lower Forms. By G. MASSEE, Kew Gardens. *With Illustrations.*

AIR AND WATER. Professor V. B. LEWES, M.A. *Illustrated.*

THE CHEMISTRY OF LIFE AND HEALTH. By C. W. KIMMINS, M.A. Camb. *Illustrated.*

THE MECHANICS OF DAILY LIFE. By V. P. SELLS, M.A. *Illustrated.*

ENGLISH SOCIAL REFORMERS. H. DE B. GIBBINS, M.A.

ENGLISH TRADE AND FINANCE IN THE SEVENTEENTH CENTURY. By W. A. S. HEWINS, B.A.

THE CHEMISTRY OF FIRE. The Elementary Principles of Chemistry. By M. M. PATTISON MUIR, M.A. *Illustrated.*

A TEXT-BOOK OF AGRICULTURAL BOTANY. By M. C. POTTER, M.A., F.L.S. *Illustrated.* 3s. 6d.

THE VAULT OF HEAVEN. A Popular Introduction to Astronomy. By R. A. GREGORY. *With numerous Illustrations.*

METEOROLOGY. The Elements of Weather and Climate. By H. N. DICKSON, F.R.S.E., F.R. Met. Soc. *Illustrated.*

A MANUAL OF ELECTRICAL SCIENCE. By GEORGE J. BURCH, M.A. *With numerous Illustrations.* 3s.

THE EARTH. An Introduction to Physiography. By EVAN SMALL, M.A. *Illustrated.*

INSECT LIFE. By F. W. THEOBALD, M.A. *Illustrated.*

ENGLISH POETRY FROM BLAKE TO BROWNING. By W. M. DIXON, M.A.

ENGLISH LOCAL GOVERNMENT. By E. JENKS, M.A., Professor of Law at University College, Liverpool.

Social Questions of To-day

Edited by H. DE B. GIBBINS, M.A.

Crown 8vo. 2s. 6d.

2/6

A series of volumes upon those topics of social, economic, and industrial interest that are at the present moment foremost in the public mind. Each volume of the series is written by an author who is an acknowledged authority upon the subject with which he deals.

The following Volumes of the Series are ready :—

TRADE UNIONISM—NEW AND OLD. By G. HOWELL, Author of 'The Conflicts of Capital and Labour.' *Second Edition.*

THE CO-OPERATIVE MOVEMENT TO-DAY. By G. J. HOLYOAKE, Author of 'The History of Co-operation.' *Second Edition.*

MUTUAL THRIFT. By Rev. J. FROME WILKINSON, M.A., Author of 'The Friendly Society Movement.'

PROBLEMS OF POVERTY : An Inquiry into the Industrial Conditions of the Poor. By J. A. HOBSON, M.A. *Third Edition.*

THE COMMERCE OF NATIONS. By C. F. BASTABLE, M.A., Professor of Economics at Trinity College, Dublin.

THE ALIEN INVASION. By W. H. WILKINS, B.A., Secretary to the Society for Preventing the Immigration of Destitute Aliens.

THE RURAL EXODUS. By P. ANDERSON GRAHAM.

LAND NATIONALIZATION. By HAROLD COX, B.A.

A SHORTER WORKING DAY. By H. DE B. GIBBINS and R. A. HADFIELD, of the Hecla Works, Sheffield.

BACK TO THE LAND : An Inquiry into the Cure for Rural Depopulation. By H. E. MOORE.

TRUSTS, POOLS AND CORNERS : As affecting Commerce and Industry. By J. STEPHEN JEANS, M.R.I., F.S.S.

THE FACTORY SYSTEM. By R. COOKE TAYLOR.

THE STATE AND ITS CHILDREN. By GERTRUDE TUCKWELL.

WOMEN'S WORK. By LADY DILKE, MISS BULLEY, and MISS WHITLEY.

MUNICIPALITIES AT WORK. The Municipal Policy of Six Great Towns, and its Influence on their Social Welfare. By FREDERICK DOLMAN.

SOCIALISM AND MODERN THOUGHT. By M. KAUF-MANN.

THE HOUSING OF THE WORKING CLASSES. By R. F. BOWMAKER.

MODERN CIVILISATION IN SOME OF ITS ECONOMIC ASPECTS. By W. CUNNINGHAM, D.D., Fellow of Trinity College, Cambridge.

Classical Translations

Edited by H. F. FOX, M.A., Fellow and Tutor of Brasenose College, Oxford.

Messrs. Methuen are issuing a New Series of Translations from the Greek and Latin Classics. They have enlisted the services of some of the best Oxford and Cambridge Scholars, and it is their intention that the Series shall be distinguished by literary excellence as well as by scholarly accuracy.

ÆSCHYLUS—Agamemnon, Chöephoroe, Eumenides. Translated by LEWIS CAMPBELL, LL.D., late Professor of Greek at St. Andrews. 5s.

CICERO—De Oratore I. Translated by E. N. P. MOOR, M.A., Assistant Master at Clifton. 3s. 6d.

CICERO—Select Orations (Pro Milone, Pro Murena, Philippic II., In Catilinam). Translated by H. E. D. BLAKISTON, M.A., Fellow and Tutor of Trinity College, Oxford. 5s.

CICERO—De Natura Deorum. Translated by F. BROOKS, M.A., late Scholar of Balliol College, Oxford. 3s. 6d.

LUCIAN—Six Dialogues (Nigrinus, Icaro-Menippus, The Cock, The Ship, The Parasite, The Lover of Falsehood). Translated by S. T. IRWIN, M.A., Assistant Master at Clifton ; late Scholar of Exeter College, Oxford. 3s. 6d.

SOPHOCLES—Electra and Ajax. Translated by E. D. A. MORSHEAD, M.A., late Scholar of New College, Oxford ; Assistant Master at Winchester. 2s. 6d.

TACITUS—Agricola and Germania. Translated by R. B. TOWNSHEND, late Scholar of Trinity College, Cambridge. 2s. 6d.

Educational Books

CLASSICAL

TACITI AGRICOLA.   With Introduction, Notes, Map, etc. By R. F. DAVIS, M.A., Assistant Master at Weymouth College. *Crown 8vo.   2s.*

TACITI GERMANIA.   By the same Editor.   *Crown 8vo.   2s.*

HERODOTUS: EASY SELECTIONS.   With Vocabulary. By A. C. LIDDELL, M.A., Assistant Master at Nottingham High School.   *Fcap. 8vo.   1s. 6d.*

SELECTIONS FROM THE ODYSSEY.   By E. D. STONE, M.A., late Assistant Master at Eton.   *Fcap. 8vo.   1s. 6d.*

PLAUTUS: THE CAPTIVI.   Adapted for Lower Forms by J. H. FREESE, M.A., late Fellow of St. John's, Cambridge.   *1s. 6d.*

DEMOSTHENES AGAINST CONON AND CALLICLES. Edited with Notes, and Vocabulary, by F. DARWIN SWIFT, M.A., formerly Scholar of Queen's College, Oxford; Assistant Master at Denstone College.   *Fcap. 8vo.   2s.*

GERMAN

A COMPANION GERMAN GRAMMAR.   By H. DE B. GIBBINS, M.A., Assistant Master at Nottingham High School. *Crown 8vo.   1s. 6d.*

GERMAN PASSAGES FOR UNSEEN TRANSLATION. By E. M'QUEEN GRAY.   *Crown 8vo.   2s. 6d.*

SCIENCE

THE WORLD OF SCIENCE.   Including Chemistry, Heat, Light, Sound, Magnetism, Electricity, Botany, Zoology, Physiology, Astronomy, and Geology.   By R. ELLIOT STEEL, M.A., F.C.S. 147 Illustrations.   *Second Edition.   Crown 8vo.   2s. 6d.*

'Mr. Steel's Manual is admirable in many ways.   The book is well calculated to attract and retain the attention of the young.'—*Saturday Review.*

'If Mr. Steel is to be placed second to any for this quality of lucidity, it is only to Huxley himself; and to be named in the same breath with this master of the craft of teaching is to be accredited with the clearness of style and simplicity of arrangement that belong to thorough mastery of a subject.'—*Parents' Review.*

ELEMENTARY LIGHT.   By R. E. STEEL.   With numerous Illustrations.   *Crown 8vo.   4s. 6d.*

ENGLISH

ENGLISH RECORDS. A Companion to the History of England. By H. E. MALDEN, M.A. *Crown 8vo.* 3s. 6d.

A book which aims at concentrating information upon dates, genealogy, officials, constitutional documents, etc., which is usually found scattered in different volumes.

THE ENGLISH CITIZEN: HIS RIGHTS AND DUTIES. By H. E. MALDEN, M.A. 1s. 6d.

'The book goes over the same ground as is traversed in the school books on this subject written to satisfy the requirements of the Education code. It would serve admirably the purposes of a text-book, as it is well based in historical facts, and keeps quite clear of party matters.'—*Scotsman.*

METHUEN'S COMMERCIAL SERIES.

Edited by H. DE B. GIBBINS, M.A.

BRITISH COMMERCE AND COLONIES FROM ELIZABETH TO VICTORIA. By H. DE B. GIBBINS, M.A., Author of 'The Industrial History of England,' etc. etc. 2s.

COMMERCIAL EXAMINATION PAPERS. By H. DE B. GIBBINS, M.A. 1s. 6d.

THE ECONOMICS OF COMMERCE. By H. DE B. GIBBINS, M.A. 1s. 6d.

A MANUAL OF FRENCH COMMERCIAL CORRESPONDENCE. By S. E. BALLY, Modern Language Master at the Manchester Grammar School. 2s.

A FRENCH COMMERCIAL READER. By S. E. BALLY. 2s.

COMMERCIAL GEOGRAPHY, with special reference to Trade Routes, New Markets, and Manufacturing Districts. By L. W. LYDE, M.A., of the Academy, Glasgow. 2s.

A PRIMER OF BUSINESS. By S. JACKSON, M.A. 1s. 6d.

COMMERCIAL ARITHMETIC. By F. G. TAYLOR, M.A. 1s. 6d.

WORKS BY A. M. M. STEDMAN, M.A.

INITIA LATINA: Easy Lessons on Elementary Accidence. *Second Edition. Fcap. 8vo. 1s.*

FIRST LATIN LESSONS. *Fourth Edition. Crown 8vo. 2s.*

FIRST LATIN READER. With Notes adapted to the Shorter Latin Primer and Vocabulary. *Second Edition. Crown 8vo. 1s. 6d.*

EASY SELECTIONS FROM CAESAR. Part I. The Helvetian War. *18mo. 1s.*

EASY SELECTIONS FROM LIVY. Part I. The Kings of Rome. *18mo. 1s. 6d.*

EASY LATIN PASSAGES FOR UNSEEN TRANSLATION. *Third Edition. Fcap. 8vo. 1s. 6d.*

EXEMPLA LATINA. First Lessons in Latin Accidence. With Vocabulary. *Crown 8vo. 1s.*

EASY LATIN EXERCISES ON THE SYNTAX OF THE SHORTER AND REVISED LATIN PRIMER. With Vocabulary. *Fourth Edition. Crown 8vo. 2s. 6d.* Issued with the consent of Dr. Kennedy

THE LATIN COMPOUND SENTENCE: Rules and Exercises. *Crown 8vo. 1s. 6d.* With Vocabulary. *2s.*

NOTANDA QUAEDAM: Miscellaneous Latin Exercises on Common Rules and Idioms. *Second Edition. Fcap. 8vo. 1s. 6d.* With Vocabulary, 2s.

LATIN VOCABULARIES FOR REPETITION: Arranged according to Subjects. *Fourth Edition. Fcap. 8vo. 1s. 6d.*

A VOCABULARY OF LATIN IDIOMS AND PHRASES. *18mo. 1s.*

STEPS TO GREEK. *18mo. 1s.*

EASY GREEK PASSAGES FOR UNSEEN TRANSLATION. *Fcap. 8vo. 1s. 6d.*

GREEK VOCABULARIES FOR REPETITION. Arranged according to Subjects. *Second Edition. Fcap. 8vo. 1s. 6d.*

GREEK TESTAMENT SELECTIONS. For the use of Schools. *Third Edition.* With Introduction, Notes, and Vocabulary. *Fcap. 8vo. 2s. 6d.*

STEPS TO FRENCH. 18mo. 8d.

FIRST FRENCH LESSONS. *Crown 8vo.* 1s.

EASY FRENCH PASSAGES FOR UNSEEN TRANSLA-
TION. *Second Edition. Fcap. 8vo.* 1s. 6d.

EASY FRENCH EXERCISES ON ELEMENTARY
SYNTAX. With Vocabulary. *Crown 8vo.* 2s. 6d.

FRENCH VOCABULARIES FOR REPETITION : Arranged
according to Subjects. *Third Edition. Fcap. 8vo.* 1s.

SCHOOL EXAMINATION SERIES.

EDITED BY A. M. M. STEDMAN, M.A.

Crown 8vo. 2s. 6d.

FRENCH EXAMINATION PAPERS IN MISCELLANE-
OUS GRAMMAR AND IDIOMS. By A. M. M. STEDMAN, M.A.
Sixth Edition.

A KEY, issued to Tutors and Private Students only, to be had on
application to the Publishers. *Second Edition. Crown 8vo.* 6s. *net.*

LATIN EXAMINATION PAPERS IN MISCELLANEOUS
GRAMMAR AND IDIOMS. By A. M. M. STEDMAN, M.A.
Fourth Edition. KEY issued as above. 6s. *net.*

GREEK EXAMINATION PAPERS IN MISCELLANEOUS
GRAMMAR AND IDIOMS. By A. M. M. STEDMAN, M.A.
Third Edition. KEY issued as above. 6s. *net.*

GERMAN EXAMINATION PAPERS IN MISCELLANE-
OUS GRAMMAR AND IDIOMS. By R. J. MORICH, Manchester. *Third Edition.* KEY issued as above. 6s. *net.*

HISTORY AND GEOGRAPHY EXAMINATION PAPERS.
By C. H. SPENCE, M.A., Clifton Coll.

SCIENCE EXAMINATION PAPERS. By R. E. STEEL, M.A.,
F.C.S., Chief Natural Science Master, Bradford Grammar School.
In two vols. Part I. Chemistry ; Part II. Physics.

GENERAL KNOWLEDGE EXAMINATION PAPERS.
By A. M. M. STEDMAN, M.A. *Second Edition.* KEY issued as
above. 7s. *net.*

9 783744 712163